Nanny ABCs

The Sitter's Handbook

*A complete alphabet
how-to guide for
every child caregiver.*

DANNY J. NANNY

DANIEL JOSEPH ROSENTHAL

Dedicated to Yve, Tej, and Stephen for making me the nanny I am.
Mom and Dad for always being my number one fans.

Printed in the United States of America

First Printing, 2019

Print ISBN: 978-1-54398-389-0

eBook ISBN: 978-1-54398-390-6

www.NannyABCs.com

ABOUT THE AUTHOR

Daniel Joseph Rosenthal, now Danny J. Nanny, began his fifteen-year career in childcare while working in the music industry. But even as a successful billboard charting songwriter and touring performer, he found himself most happy off the stage, where he mentored children as the director of the Skokie Park District's circus summer day camp. In 2018, he launched his summer time passion into a full-time career, beginning his journey as a nanny. Rosenthal has traveled internationally with his nanny families, recognized for his outstanding performance by Chicago Collegiate Nannies, and his expertise has been featured on Care.com. In addition to working as a full-time nanny, Rosenthal teaches a course for beginning nannies. In this A-Z alphabet how-to handbook, Rosenthal addresses the most common challenges every nanny, sitter, and parent face, while sharing his passion for excellence in the field of childcare. For more information visit NannyABCs.com

FORWARD

As an agency owner and former nanny, I often struggle with finding an unbiased voice to address both families and nannies alike when it comes to industry best practices. Danny J. Nanny is that voice. Danny has cultivated his childcare expertise through working with children in many different capacities and settings. His no-nonsense approach in *Nanny ABCs* relates well to novice nannies while reinforcing professional policy and procedure with seasoned nannies. *Nanny ABCs* is an important tool for families who do not have the time or forethought to address individual training topics with new-hires and for nannies who want to grow within their industry.

Nanny ABCs flawlessly covers topics every nanny should know from A to Z in a way that is clear, concise and immediately applicable. In an industry that is prone to relativism and opinion, Danny presents an objective voice that holds both families and nannies to common standards. I cannot recommend this book highly enough and appreciate the work that Danny has done to establish benchmark practices within the childcare industry.

Lydia Brown, founder of Boston Collegiate Nannies &
Chicago Collegiate Nannies

INTRODUCTION

I'm proud to be providing answers for situations every nanny and sitter, like myself, encounter. I wish I had something like this when I started nannying but it didn't exist, so I wrote it."

Danny J. Nanny

Nannying is a rewarding and worthwhile career. It is different from being a parent, a teacher, a daycare employee, or a camp counselor. There is, of course, some crossover but being proficient in any of those roles alone will not make someone the best nanny. Furthermore, nannying is more than just a college job or a placeholder profession. Quality nannying requires more. It takes a special person with a unique personality.

When I first became a nanny, I found little-to-no information on the obstacles I'd face. I learned on the job the necessity of being an authority on laundry, as well as chef for children – and their parents! I discovered most parents need guidance on how to be employers. I learned the balance between employer and friend is often a fragile one.

I had a rocky start as a nanny. In my first position caring for a 2-year-old girl and her 4-year-old brother, I immediately discovered a big problem, one every nanny faces: How do nannies handle their bathroom needs in public? I searched the internet. I read forums. I read parenting books. I didn't find the answer. Like most nannies, I figured it out on my own. In this book, I cover topics like these so the next generation of nannies don't have to learn the hard way.

Unfortunately, my potty query wasn't the end of my questions on how to be a great nanny. I continually hit dead ends while searching for answers to everyday nanny challenges. When I did find a book written by a nanny, it was often a book on parenting. That was disappointing. Why not a how-to-nanny book?

This book is intended to help nannies and sitters, at any level, looking for guidance, and for parents and agencies seeking to better prepare their nannies for the reality of this wonderful profession. This book covers the nanny industry's best practices and answers those questions I encountered during my first year as a nanny. My hope is this book helps you on your journey to making the most of a rewarding and invaluable career in childcare.

Danny J. Nanny

ADVICE

From a 12-year-old baby-sitter to a seasoned nanny, navigating the terrain of a professional child caregiver is complex and far from easy. Unknowns lie around every corner and it is up to the nanny to treat every issue with mindfulness. From time to time, I've been privy to wonderful guidance that has lifted my performance as nanny to the next level.

"Everything is a treat." - Nicole Lumsden, Nanny

It is not only difficult, but it is near impossible to meet some children's expectations of constant desserts, new toys, and to be nonstop entertained. Charges, children in the care of a nanny, become humbler, more understanding, and more empathetic when their mindsets are shifted from expecting things to valuing every opportunity.

"Part of a nanny's work is to give parents an opportunity to share quality time with their children." - Lydia Brown, Chicago Collegiate Nannies & Boston Collegiate Nannies Founder

Handing charges back to their parents at the end of the day should be more than a simple goodbye. A great nanny should be able to lift some of life's many burdens off the principals' shoulders so they can spend a little extra quality time with their children. Do an extra load of laundry or wash the dishes if you have extra time so the principals can focus on their children instead of chores.

AGENTS AND AGENCIES

Rock stars, movie stars, and nannies all have one thing in common... Agents.

An agent or agency is the conduit between a job opportunity and the talent. Nannies do not work for agencies. Agencies represent both nannies and families and perform as a matchmaker to help both parties find the best fit for success.

Agencies can help shape which characteristics a family is looking for in a nanny. Agencies can also help nannies figure out what it is they are looking for in families. Many families have never taken on the responsibility of employing a nanny before and don't realize the pitfalls. Agencies can help guide families to better understand what they must provide a nanny and how to best set them up for success. From hours per week, paid time off, and health insurance, to questions such as will the nanny need to drive, and if so, who is providing the car? Both nanny and family must think about each other's needs.

Most agencies require a nanny to have verifiable two to three years working with children (previous nanny positions, daycare, or camp leader experience), ability to make a one-year commitment, pass a background check, have a clean driving record, and be legally allowed to work in the US. Some agencies provide nannies with orientation and First Aid/CPR classes.

There is no need to worry if you find a listing for a position posted directly by a family without an agent. Many families with legitimate nanny positions choose to navigate obtaining a nanny without the help of an agency.

APPS

It seems like there is a phone app for nearly everything these days. Here are the apps that have made my life easier as a nanny.

Alarm & Timer

Don't be late! It is easy to lose track of time or become distracted with any number of tasks but staying on schedule and keeping potty accidents at bay is as easy as setting those alarms for both you and charges.

Calendar

No matter which calendar app you use, keeping track of appointments, playdates, and your work schedule is a must. Find which app works best for you to keep all your dates in once place. A shareable calendar, such as Google Cal, works great for nannies and their principals to collaborate.

Driversnote

Many families seek a nanny that owns a car and is willing to use it on the job. Principals will then offer to reimburse nannies for the mileage used.

I have tried many mileage tracking apps and Driversnote is my favorite. Press start and Driversnote immediately starts tracking the miles driven and route. Driversnote can provide a spread sheet detailing the starting and finishing points, total miles, and total reimbursement when it is time to send it to the principals. Driversnote lets the user choose whether to turn it on themselves each time or have it automatically activated every time they step in the car while other similar apps keep your location tracker on all the time, draining your phone's battery.

Maps

Bookmark the principle's home, their favorite convenience and grocery store, and the charge's school so you never have to worry about how to get there.

Pinterest

Look no further for the best app for crafts, playtime, and learning inspirations.

Quip

Quip is a personal favorite but any list making app that can easily be shared between the nanny and the principals will do the trick. Effortlessly collaborate to add or remove items for to-dos and groceries with Quip.

Yelp

Yelp is widely known for user reviews of restaurants and businesses but it is also a nanny's secret weapon. Read reviews, post reviews, and bookmark playgrounds, indoor play spaces, and museums for you and your charge to visit.

Employment

These are the go-to caregiver platforms to look for full time and part time positions, as well as one off babysitting gigs.
- *Caregiver (the sitter's side for Care.com).*
- *Sittercity.*
- *Urban Sitter.*

ASSERTIVE

Speaking up and communicating needs to principals can be difficult for nannies. Every nanny is confronted with nerve wracking topics, such as scheduling and payment, that can be troublesome to bring up to their employer. I have found in difficult times that there is no one else to advocate for your needs except for yourself. Standing up for yourself is not easy but becomes easier each time and shows passion for your work.

BAD WORDS

Poor listening and bad behavior sit at the top of most principal's list of challenges they face with their children. Still, swearing is about the most shocking. It can be a mystery how these horrible words came out of the sweetest little faces and figuring out what to do next without setting you and your charge back can be difficult. Luckily, there are solutions.

Did You Hear What You Thought You Heard?

Many charges do not curse on purpose. Some appropriate words sound remarkably close to naughty ones when they come from the mouth of a child learning to speak.

Good Words and Bad Words

There are neither bad nor good words until charges learn that words have connotations. Make sure both nanny and the principals are on the same page when it comes to which words are not allowed in the household.

The Origin Mystery of Bad Words

Don't spend too much time getting Scooby Doo and the Mystery Gang together to solve the case. The origin of a swear probably didn't come from someone inside the home anyway. A 2009 study 'Taboo or Not Taboo?' revealed most bad language comes from children's peers and the media. Children are sponges and will soak up their surroundings. Bottomline, do not to swear around children.

Powerful Reactions

The feedback children receive when they use words will influence if and when they use them again. It will be an uphill battle if an adult's first reaction to a child's swearing is laughter or alarm. Do yourself a favor and make the first reaction calm.

Alternative Words

Give charges alternative, household approved, words to replace swears. Alternate words work so well because it falls in line with many experiences children already have, such as getting corrected on pronunciation and being told they mean to use a different word. Switch out "stupid" with "silly". Replacing words is a mighty tool to get children to stop cursing.

BATHROOMS

Using the Bathroom at Home

If a child can tell an adult they need their bottom wiped it is time to show them how to do it for themselves.

1. Show charges how many pieces of toilet paper they need and have them rip it.
   - I tell my charges to use two to three pieces of toilet paper, but that is up to you. Make a removable line on the wall for a charge to measure the toilet paper if they cannot count.
   - Let charges know toilet paper is not something to be wasted. Have charges roll the toilet paper back if they unroll too much or put the toilet paper aside for them to use later if they rip off more than enough.
2. Trade off with team work.
   - Wipe your charge once to show them exactly what to do, where the toilet paper should go, and how it should feel. Then have your charge try. Now take turns until their bottom is all clean.

Starting a child on bathroom independence can open up some emotional bonding feelings for children and adults. It can be extremely difficult to stop helping a charge with something you've done for them their entire life. Likewise, children may do whatever it takes to continue being coddled. It will be challenging as some children may beg, say they are scared, or don't know how. Charges may even say that it hurts their feelings that you are no longer there for them. While this may hurt your heart, it starts to cultivate a new type of relationship where charges get your attention from positive behavior instead of any behavior.

It takes two things for charges to become bathroom independent.

1. Encouragement.
   - Every step of the way say, "good job," "I know you can do it," and "I'm so proud of you."
2. Giving Charges Space.
   - When this process begins charges will be slow. You may even want to step in and do it for them but let charges

take their time and learn how to take care of themselves. It will be worth the time and effort for everyone.

- Give charges space and leave if they begin pretending that using the bathroom by themselves is too hard for them. Simply say, "I know you can do it. I'll be back in a little bit. Let me know when you're ready for me to double check for you."

- Learning to use the bathroom by oneself is a process. Really let them give it a go. Charges will soon stop asking for help and take care of business themselves.

Using the Bathroom in Public

You gotta go when you gotta go. It is never easy for nannies to use the bathroom when they are out and about in public with charges. Nannies have to wrangle charges to come with. They don't want to go. And you may not know where bathrooms are if you're traveling.

Like most people, you will naturally be nervous to attempt going to the bathroom in front of other people; even more so in front of charges. At first, I wasn't sure what to do when my charges and I were on the town and I was faced with my own potty emergency. My head would fill with thoughts of, "how long can I hold it," and "I know can't leave them outside the stall." I searched the internet for what to do but ultimately, I had to figure out what works for me.

Just like most things, going to the bathroom with charges starts with a basic routine. Every situation is going to be different but I've traveled the world with my charges and while bathrooms are not the same everywhere, our routine worked every time.

1. Potty Breaks are for Everyone, Even Nannies.

- Nannies may be used to corralling charges to come together and use the facilities but this is also your chance to utilize the washroom.

2. Have charges use the toilet first.

3. It is the nanny's turn to use the toilet.
   - Leaving young charges outside the stall is not an option. Still, privacy is important but easier to accomplish than you might let yourself believe. Children understand privacy because sometimes they want privacy too. Simply ask your charges to stand on the other side of the stall and turn to face away from you. Try giving your charges an activity or keep a conversation going if that makes it easier to keep them for wandering around the stall.

4. Let the charge know you need privacy. It doesn't have to be a long conversation. I've found, "Ok, it's my turn to use the bathroom and I need some privacy so please stand on that side and turn away."

5. Everyone washes their hands.

BATTLES

There are endless uphill battles from challenging picky eaters to try new foods or asking a charge to clean their room, and it can be defeating when things aren't going the nanny's way.

Give those challenges a break if you begin to find yourself adding unneeded hassle. There is absolutely nothing wrong with letting everything go back to the normal for a few days or a week to recharge and gain perspective. More than "pick your battles", "pick when you battle."

BITING & HITTING

Children bite and hit before they develop self-control and the skills to better communicate their needs. The reasons can range from releasing teething pain, gaining control in a situation, attention, acting in defense, and expressing emotions that they may have trouble understanding, such as confusion, exhaustion, or hunger.

Infants Biting Expectations

It is inevitable that infants are going to put their mouth on things. Biting is a baby's sixth sense, an extension of touch and taste. Babies bite to explore the world around them. Infants will need a significant amount of help from adults and childproofing to determine what is and isn't appropriate to bite. It is important to recognize that infants do not realize that biting hurts others.

Infant Biting Solutions

Clean and chilled washcloths or teething rings kept in the refrigerator will go a long way to teach an infant what is appropriate to bite. This will also relieve any teething pain and aid their much-needed oral stimulation.

Toddler Biting & Hitting Expectations

Toddlers are quick to change emotions and do whatever makes sense to them in the moment. However, by the time a child is a toddler they are beginning to learn that principals and caregivers can support and comfort them through their tough moments.

Toddler Biting & Hitting Prevention

Children begin to name their feelings when they become toddlers. This gives principals and caregivers the opportunity to validate their emotions and guide them to a desired response. Helping toddlers learn to identify their moods and name their emotions will help steer them towards effective solutions: weaning them from biting and hitting others.

Self-soothing begins during infancy. Toddlerhood is the beginning of self-regulating emotions and discovering ways to respond to difficult moments, such as distancing themselves from situations that upset them. Encourage those moments. Sometimes it is best to let charges storm off when they are upset, self sooth, and come back when they are ready.

Toddler Biting & Hitting Solutions

Make it clear to a charge with eye contact, a firm and calm voice that biting and hitting is not ok. Then reassure them that there are other appropriate ways to express the difficulty they are having.

Help younger charges learn to communicate their wants and needs. Remind charges the appropriate words and actions you would like them to use. Teach charges key words and phrases such as, "no, thank you," and "please stop," to help them set boundaries for themselves.

Let charges know how proud you are of them for transition from biting and hitting to telling, showing, or using other coping skills because it did not come easy. Give charges the praise they deserve.

BUDGET

Always ask the principals if there is a budget for activities, outings, crafts, and necessities when starting off with a family. The outcome can vary from the principals opting to have every expenditure itemized, to being completely hands off. No matter how expenses are handled, having an idea of how the family would prefer their nanny to deal with expenses will aid in planning the fun for the days, weeks, and months ahead.

CAMERAS

Nanny Cam

A nanny camera is a security and safety device used to monitor and record the home, children and caregiver. Home cameras come in a wide variety of visible and hidden. "Nanny cams" are becoming increasingly standard because of the ease of use and low-price points now available.

Legality

It is legal in all 50 states for a property owner or employer to video record their property and nanny without a nanny's consent. However, it is illegal to place a camera in an area a nanny has a reasonable expectation of privacy such as a bathroom or a nanny's live-in accommodations. Federal Wire Tapping laws forbid voice recording anyone without consent and while many cameras record audio it would not be admissible in a court room setting.

If you are uncomfortable with the cameras, be open and express your concerns to your employer. Ask the questions you need to put your mind at ease. "Where are the cameras located," or "how do you use the cameras?" Most employers understand that it is hard for an employee to do a good job when they feel uncomfortable. Opening up a dialogue may help everyone relax.

Before pointing out any legalities to an employer it is best to approach the subject of surveillance casually. Using legal jargon instantly takes the subject to the next level and may leave the principals feeling attacked and accused of something they are legally allowed to do.

Before I worked in homes with security cameras, I didn't think they would bother me but I came to find out they did. I felt that my privacy was being intruded because I didn't know for what purposes they were being used. Was I being watched all the time? Would the principals come home and watch them? So, I started an open discussion with the principals about the cameras and expressed my concerns. I discovered the cameras were used sparingly, usually to observe the length of their child's nap. They also told me that they would be open to taking them down, which I saw as unnecessary. Afterwards all my stress was relieved.

CHARGE /CHÄRJ/ NOUN

1. A person committed into the care of another.
2. The caregiver industry's term for the child a nanny is responsible for.

Some caregivers refer to the children they are responsible for as their Nanny Child or NC.

CHORES

It is never too early to get children involved with household chores. Incorporating charges and chores can be as simple as folding laundry while charges play nearby. Chores help children grow up with a strong sense of family and community by helping out around the home.

Encourage charges when they want to help out. No matter their age, children want to be a part of the action, even if that action is laundry. Give charges a wash cloth or towel and show them how to fold.

Chores for Toddlers

- Matching socks.
- Folding napkins.
- Folding clothes.
- Wiping tables (give charges the spray bottle).
- Unloading the dishwasher.
- Putting away clothes.
- Sweeping.
- Making beds.

Reminders

- Chores do not have to be perfect and they probably aren't going to be. The key is to get charges to help out and feel a sense of community.
- When charges start helping out at a young age, they see chores as a way of life, not an inconvenience.
- Children catch on fast and become fantastic at any task if they are given space and time to practice and learn.
- Chores can be fun. Some chores can be a race but remind charges that neatness counts.

CLEANING

Cleaning up can feel like a burden but I firmly believe that it doesn't have to be a chore. To me, cleaning up is the last part of every activity.

I love order and a tidy home but not everyone feels that way. Homes and the mess within them are very personal.

Order: Every item having a place in a home, which is decided by the people who live there.

Order is not one size fits all. Some people postulate that they thrive in a mess and will point out that they know where everything is and that is ok. While it might not be tidy, it does have order. However, it may be difficult for principals to understand that their home is a nanny's work place and some order and cleanliness must be agreed to.

Clean: Free from dirt, marks, or stains.

Generally, laundry, dishes, and surfaces all need a certain amount of daily attention to keep them in good shape. It is a good bet that if a family needs a nanny, they also need a little help keeping their home clean.

Light House Work

Be cautious of the phrase "light house work." Many employers list light house work as part of the nanny duties but it isn't exactly a well-defined phrase, rather, light house work is specific to each home.

Think of "light house work" as the daily tasks which a particular household deems necessary. People commonly wash their dishes, do a load of laundry, and wipe down the kitchen surfaces, but if a family feels their bedding must be changed every day then expect to include that as part of the "light house work" for their home.

I feel strongly that a nanny's priority should be their charges. Some principals accidentally pile loads of house work onto their nanny because nannies do a fantastic job getting things done, but it may be too much. If house work is getting in the way or overtaking your child care responsibilities, let your employer know so they can figure out a solution or adjust their needs.

COMPARING

It is very natural to compare the way in which you were raised to the life of your charge and the parenting style you may be working in, but leave your judgement at the door. Every family is different and there is no right way to raise a child. Having respect for the ways the principles parent is part of a nanny's key to success.

COMPENSATION

Standard Wage

Salaries and hourly wages for nannies differ based on area, experience (years as a nanny), responsibilities (amount of charges and duties), and live-in vs. live-out.

The International Nanny Association's 2017 Salary and Benefit Survey determined the US national average rate for nannies is $19.14/hour.

Full Time: $19.14

Live-in: $16.75

Live-out: $19.14

Part Time: $17.80

Live-in nannies usually exchange their "room" costs for a slightly lower rate per hour.

The highest paying states on average for nannies are California at $23/hour, Washington at $22/hour, and New York, Massachusetts, and Maryland at $20/hour.

As of May, 2019, Zip Recruiter determined the United States' national average annual salary for nannies to be $32,600.

Overtime

58% of nannies receive overtime as determined by the International Nanny Association's 2017 Salary and Benefit Survey. Overtime is usually counted as time and a half, for working beyond 40 hours.

Raise

Asking for a raise is asking to be compensated fairly for what you are worth. The rule of thumb is to wait 6 months to a year before asking for a raise to prove your value. Similarly, it is also appropriate to approach the conversation of a raise when the job description has changed: adding frequent trips, taking on additional house manager responsibilities, or the addition of a charge.

Payment "Under the Table"

Being paid "under the table" or without paying taxes is a red flag. Aside from it being illegal, it is a sign the family or nanny may be less than professional. If they aren't going to follow the law, can you be sure they are going to follow through with anything else they have agreed to?

Getting paid in cash or personal check might seem like a slam dunk when the nanny receives a bit more take-home pay but it ends up being a nightmare when a family refuses or forgets to pay and leaves nannies with little recourse.

Other negatives include:

- Nannies are unable to file for unemployment, secure a loan, or rent a living space because there is no record of employment.

- Families risk potential workers compensation lawsuits if a nanny is injured on the job.

- IRS fines or jail time for tax fraud.

CONSISTENCY

Consistency is king. A nanny's reaction should be the same more often than not if bad behaviors are going to improve. Charges that face the same consequences for their actions are less likely to test the limits. If screaming equals a time out one day then it better be a time out the next day. Consistency is a challenge because so much can happen so fast and we want our reactions to be ones we can stand behind.

CRAFTS

From a piece of paper and a fist full of crayons to themed gifts, crafts are much more than a rainy-day activity. Aside from a fun and productive way to spend some time, crafts nurture a charge's focus, enhance creativity, advance decision making, and increase fine motor skills.

Crafts do not need to be hard or take much time, crafting can take a few minutes or an entire day. Finding the perfect craft for a charge is a few internet searches and clicks away. Use the internet to get inspired by searching the child's age and an interest or an upcoming celebration or holiday.

No one is born knowing how to use a glue stick, hold a pencil, or guide scissors. Use crafting as a path to encourage a child to try new things and learn.

DATE NIGHT

Whether it is the first or hundredth time you are babysitting for a family there are always things to clarify with principals to improve everyone's experience.

Arrival

The standard is to arrive a few minutes before the sitting begins to get settled and use the washroom. No one feels Elin Hilderbrand's "to be early is to be on time," any stronger than a parent waiting for a sitter.

Confirm Hours

It is important to eliminate any miscommunication by confirming in person how long your services will be needed even if you have already confirmed through a text or an email. Confirming hours also opens up the dialogue for some parents to ask if you are comfortable staying longer. Confirming the hours is especially important if you already have a time you must leave or have plans in place for someone to pick you up when the night is over.

Confirm Medical Needs

Medical needs range far and wide. A child may need to take a medication with dinner or have a bandage replaced before bed. It is best to have the complete picture in written directions so you are able to provide the best care for that child.

Confirm the Pay Rate

It may feel uncomfortable to bring up how much you charge but it is important to eliminate confusion at the get go instead of finding out at the end that there is a discrepancy.

Do Not Leave Without Being Paid

Sitters that leave without being paid, even when they are assured by principals they will be, often regret it. It is ok to wait and confirm a principal's payment on your end before departing for the evening. Once a sitter leaves there is little action they can take.

Exchange Numbers

If you haven't already, exchange numbers with the principals. Find out who is the best and next best people to contact in an emergency.

Questions

It often feels like there is so much to go through when babysitting for a family and so little time. Families are constantly evolving and trying new things, be it a later bed time or new rules on screen time. Best practice is for babysitters to go over their standard questions every time they arrive.

- *What are the rules of the house?*

- *What are the rules for screen time?*

- *When is bed time?*

- *What is the bedtime routine? (Knowing the basics of a child's bedtime routine will allow for a smooth transition.)*

- *What would you like us to do for meals and when are meal times?*

- *Does anyone have any medical needs or allergies?*

- *Where is the first aid kit?*

- *What and who are the emergency contacts?*

- *What is the internet password?*

- *Is there anything you would like us to accomplish?*

- *What time should I expect you to return?*

DISCIPLINE

Often times being a nanny means inheriting, transitioning to your way, or adding onto the ways the previous nanny and principals' discipline. Children realize you are a different person and whether they like the way you do things or not they will adjust their behavior for you.

- *Stay calm.*

- *Remain firm.*

- *Acknowledge the charge's feelings.*

- *Give a warning.*

- *Explain the consequences of the actions.*

- *Do not ask principals to enforce your punishments.*

- *Involve principals when necessary.*

It is common for nannies and charges to have a fantastic day until a principal arrives. Then a show of "everything is going wrong" starring the charge begins. Principals are generally aware of this. Paying little attention to the show helps discourage the pretend drama. The pretend drama may also occur when the nanny arrives.

DISHWASHER

The dishwasher is the greatest invention since before sliced bread but not every dish or utensil can survive the detergent, rinse cycle, or heat of a dishwasher. Learn what a dishwasher can't handle before ruining a principal's 15-year-old sentimental wooden spoon, like I did.

Do Not Place Wood in the Dishwasher

Never place wooden spoons, spatulas, cutting boards or anything with a wooden handle into the dishwasher. The heat used to dry will warp or worse, crack the wooden items in the machine.

Do Not Place Cast-Iron in the Dishwasher

Placing cast iron in the dishwasher will more than strip away the seasoning, it may cause the cookware to rust. Instead scrub it with warm water and dry it right away. Easily re-season cast iron cookware by rubbing a teaspoon or less of oil (olive, canola, etc.) with your finger around the cast iron cooking surface. Then place it on the stove and heat it. Turn off the heat once it begins to smoke and it is ready to go.

Do Not Place Aluminum in the Dishwasher

While technically it can be washed in a dishwasher, the cookware will oxidize and fade over many washes. Look up what the manufacturer says or ask the principal if you're uncertain before placing any items in the dishwasher.

Do Not Place Noble Metals in the Dishwasher

The dishwasher's chemical detergents can corrode the shiny finishes of copper, silver, gold, and bronze.

Do Not Place Nonstick Cookware in the Dishwasher

The nonstick of a nonstick pan can sometimes disintegrate after a thorough wash from a dishwasher. However, you may be in luck and able to save a few minutes if the manufacturer labels it dishwasher safe.

Do Not Place Plastic in the Dishwasher

It is best to place dishwasher safe plastics on the top rack. Still, they may become scratched or dull over time. Be careful, not every manufacturer puts a permanent label into their plastics to warn the consumer which plastics will melt and which will survive the dishwasher's cycle.

Do Not Place Knives in the Dishwasher

The harsh dishwasher detergents cause fine knife blades to dull while the heat causes the blade to expand and contrast loosening it from its handle. Knives in the dishwasher are also a possible cut waiting to happen when it is time to unload the dishwasher.

Do Not Place Acrylic in the Dishwasher

Cute, lightweight and colorful acrylic dishes can hairline fracture and fade when run through a dishwasher.

Do Not Place Heirlooms in the Dishwasher

Chips, fading, and disintegrating a finish is likely when delicate items such as fine china, crystal, and anything handprinted or sentimental are run through the dishwasher as a dishwasher's cycle and detergent are unforgiving. If you're wondering, I fixed the wooden spoon with a food safe FDA approved edible wood glue and my employer's ok.

DON'T MAKE IT PERSONAL

Nanny & charge and nanny & principal relationships are complicated. Nannying is a job and it should not define you as a person.

Nanny & Charge

The ups and downs of childhood are taxing. For children, when fun isn't being had it may seem like it will never happen again. Children wear their emotions on their sleeve and have little to no inner monologue. If something isn't going their way, they will be sure to let everyone know.

I have overheard my charge whisper to himself, "Danny isn't my friend," when he thought I was being unfair, but he is three years-old and it wasn't meant for me to hear or get upset from. Not every bad feeling a charge has is a provocation, so let it go. If the same comes from an older charge they may want you to hear it but acknowledging it gives them the power so, again, let it go.

Whether charges know it or not, a nanny is often the perfect target to take disappointment out on. There is no shield to protect any caregiver from being in the "no man's land" of a child's frustration. Sometimes the best any nanny can do is let the emotions roll away like water off a duck's back and remember tomorrow is a new day.

Nanny & Principal

A principal may want the nanny to feel like part of the family but the reality is even a live-in nanny isn't actually part of the family. A nanny's purpose isn't to become part of the family but to care, nurture, and look after it. Thinking that you are part of the family can lead to heartache, especially if the nanny is the only one who feels that way.

Some principals have no option but to bring work or the stress of a hard day home with them. Live-in or not, nannies are a part of a family's home life and there isn't always a good way for a nanny to avoid its struggles. Nannies can get caught in the crossfires of a domestic dispute. Stay out of it and do not take sides. You may need to remind the principals that it isn't your place to align yourself with or judge other members of the family.

When you find yourself bringing your nanny work life home with you it is definitely time to do something for yourself. Make plans, call a friend, take a spa day, or have a slice of cake, whatever you need to bring a smile to work tomorrow.

DUTIES

Before committing to a family, nannies must decide what care and responsibilities they are comfortable providing. Nannies should consider where they have knowledge, skills, and what they are willing to learn for the position. On the flip side, families must also take into account what nanny duties are on their wish list and which duties are realistically performed by a nanny. Positions vary and the bulk of responsibilities are determined by how many children there are to care for and their ages.

Possible Nanny Duties

- *Rinsing dishes.*

- *Loading & unloading dishwasher.*

- *Wiping down kitchen and dining room surfaces.*

- *Sweeping & vacuuming.*

- *Changing children's/family's laundry and bedding.*

- *Preparing meals and snacks for charges.*

- *Preparing dinners for the entire family.*

- *Keeping family areas tidy.*

- *Pick up/drop off children to school and after school activities.*

- *Creating age appropriate activities and crafts.*

- *Bathing and dressing children.*

- *Changing diapers.*

- *Potty training.*

- *Sleep training.*

- *Homework help.*

- *Organizing areas of the home.*

The list can go on and on. While the quantity of tasks a nanny is willing to perform may put them in high demand, a nanny who performs only a few duties with superb quality may also make them more valuable to families.

EMERGENCIES

Have a plan, the emergency contact list, and be ready to call 911 if a situation calls for it. Emergencies vary but the concept remains the same. Emergencies require a caregiver to act swiftly and calmly to keep charges safe then contact and update the principals.

Prevent an Emergency

Before accepting any nanny or sitter position be prepared to get training to fully understand the medical needs required of the charges you will be watching. Ask to be trained on any conditions, medication, and devices you will regularly use or may have to use in an emergency. Training on medical conditions should include what the condition is, how it is being treated, and any symptoms to be aware of.

Be Prepared

A "go bag" or backpack is a wonderful accessory to pack the usual basic items. Always have a first aid kit and a charge's medication within reach.

Becoming First Aid and CPR certified is a true benefit, giving nannies expertise and a method to navigate those common and extreme situations. Plus, most nanny positions require it. For more information on First Aid and CPR certification, see "H" for Health.

Many emergencies are prevented by being vigilant when watching your charges. If something is making you uncomfortable, save yourself the pain of regret and pull the charge out from the situation. You are in control; these children are your responsibility, and that is that.

ENCOURAGEMENT

Pep talks, cheering, and high fives are some of the best forms of encouragement. There is no better push to achieve a goal than a reminder that you possess the strength to persevere from someone that cares.

Children benefit from having a cheerleader to hit milestones. Just like anyone, children become used to having certain things done for them and are less than likely to jump at the chance to become a little bit more independent. It is important to take a step back every now and again and explain to a charge how to perform a task and then cheer the little one on. Encouragement is completely free, easy to give, and never goes out style.

My Favorites Encouragement Tools

- *Thumbs Up.*
  Just as good as a high five, a thumbs up is a fabulous way to encourage children. A thumbs up may even be better than a high five because they can be given from a distance.

- *Nanny Points.*
  Even though nanny points (Danny J. Nanny Points) can't be exchanged for prizes they are super fun to get. Children go bananas for nanny points. Start giving out nanny points and

charges will begin to beg to perform a chore to get some of those sweet, sweet nanny points.

EXPECTATIONS

High or low, no matter where expectations are set, they must be made clear or they become unreachable. It can be hard to vocalize and set the finish line for success; even more so for children because expectations continue to grow as they age.

Communication

No matter where the expectation goal posts are planted, the solution is to continually talk through situations that are about to arise. Many times, children seem out of control when they just haven't been told what is expected of them. Whether it's a doctor's office, school, or flying on a plane, entering a new place is scary. Take away the surprises and tell charges what there is to look forward to. In the same vein, if you are unsure what lies ahead ask the principals to set your expectations.

Make a Game Plan

If you are going to a movie theater make sure to tell your charges that you expect them to be silent and whisper to you if they need something. Remember you set the expectation bar and you can raise it.

EXPENSES

Some families will prefer to reimburse their nanny while others will set the nanny up with a family credit card. In the same vein, some caregivers will hesitate to pay for expense up front even if they are assured they will be paid back. No matter the method, it is up to the principals and nanny to figure out what works for both parties when it comes to possible out of pocket expenses for the nanny. Expenses are going to come up and it is important to put everyone's mind at ease by working out the details beforehand.

FINDING THE RIGHT FIT

The phrase, "finding the right fit," comes up a lot in the nanny industry, and unsurprisingly many careers. It simply means that the family a nanny works for reflects their own values, interests, and finds it easy to collaborate. A family that travels extensively deserves a nanny who loves to travel. A routine motivated family needs a well-organized caregiver. Likewise, if a family is disorganized, an incredibly thorough nanny will be driven nuts.

Steps to Finding the Right Fit

- *Assess Your Own Assets.*
  Can you cook? Are you crafty? Do you enjoy pretend play? Answering these questions begins to point a nanny in the direction of the family they are most compatible with and who can most benefit from their unique talents. A nanny that knows their way around a kitchen will be a huge asset to a family that needs help with meals. A crafty nanny who enjoys playing pretend may want to work with younger aged children.

- *Be Clear and Ask the Family Questions During the Interview.*
Always ask questions during the interview to limit and avoid confusion between what the family is expecting and the position's realities. Similar to buying a home, a family has their nanny wish list and then they have their must haves. Nannies should also have an idea of what their needs are as well as what they are willing to do and what they believe they can learn.

  Be up front and clear with a family in the interview process. Before you leave the interview make sure the family understands where you are and are not flexible in regards to compensation and performing duties a family is looking for.

- *Understand Your Role*
Some nanny positions seem to have it all except for a few issues here and there. No family or nanny is going to be perfect 100% of the time. Being a nanny is hard and often demanding. There may be tears some days. Understanding the role of a nanny is truly important. Nannies are not a member of the family. Still, that doesn't mean it won't feel like a nanny is part of the family, it can. Furthermore, it is wonderful for a nanny to feel a deep connection with the family they work for. However, children grow up and families' needs change. A nanny's objective is to fulfill their duties and provide a family with a sense of stability.

FIRST DAY

It doesn't matter the industry or occupation, the first days on the job can be scary for everyone. First days are the start of an adjustment period.

Hooray! A New Perspective Enters the Home

A family is super lucky to have a new set of eyes on them. New nannies can assess where the family is and help bring them to the next level.

Families and their nannies fall into habits. Often times nannies treat growing toddlers a bit younger than they are by doing things for them. It is faster to do things like dressing and feeding charges but at the cost of forgetting to instill independence and manners.

When I arrived, day one, I saw my two-year-old charge wasn't doing anything for himself. The principals and former nanny couldn't see how capable he was. So, I provided him a path toward independence.

Notes

On the first day, week, and month, there is so much to do and so little time. Face time with principals can be limited, so ask as many questions as possible on the first day and get clarification throughout the week.

Bring a note pad and be ready to take notes. It is easy to take notes on our phones but it can seem disrespectful. If having notes on your phone is your preference take notes on a pad or in a note book and transfer them to a phone after work.

Notes should focus on how tasks are currently performed, the daily schedule, and anything particular to this family. Bring a list of questions to your first day.

Example Questions

- *What is the Internet password?*
- *How are guests and deliveries buzzed in?*
- *What are the codes needed to operate the house (ex. doors)?*
- *Where are the baby lock keys?*

- *How do the lights and window shades operate?*
- *What foods does the charges and family enjoy?*
- *How do you prefer laundry to be done? (ex. separated, folded?)*

For more guidance see "N" for Notes.

Confirm the Responsibilities

The first week is the best time to reiterate and confirm the responsibility, hours, and tasks of the position with the principals.

One of the hardest parts of being a nanny is advocating for yourself. Be open to new tasks but speak up if you are uncomfortable. Asking is the first step to getting clarification, guidance and support you need to perform at your best. You want to do a fantastic job and principals want the best from their new nanny too.

Adjusting

A new person in the home is a huge change. Until a nanny's first day it may not be apparent just how different having a new nanny is going to affect the principals and charges.

Everything runs like clockwork. It doesn't matter if a nanny is replacing another or becoming a family's first, there was a prior system in place and it is now being disturbed. At first, you may feel like you are standing in someone else's shadow, but soon everyone will realize you are a different person with your own unique perspective and wonderful way of doing things.

Be Excited

Stepping through a family's front door for the first time marks a new chapter for you and the whole family and that deserves to be celebrated.

G

GAMES

Aside from having pure fun, games are a fun way for children to learn problem solving skills, how to follow directions, work as a team, develop body coordination, and exercise.

Tag

Tag is a two or more player game, best played outdoors because space to run is key.

One person is deemed the 'It' and their job is to tag (touch) another player. When the next player is tagged by 'It' they now become 'It' and tries to tag another player.

Flashlight Tag

Flashlight Tag is a two or more player game; played in the dark, either indoors with the lights off or outdoors at night.

One player is decided to be 'It' and is armed with a flashlight that remains on at all times. 'It' counts to 60; giving everyone a chance to hide. After 60 seconds the search begins. When 'It' shines the flashlight on someone and identifies them that person becomes 'It' and is handed the flashlight. The new 'It' counts to 60, giving the former 'It' a chance to hide.

Hide and Seek

Hide and Seek is a two or more player game that can be played indoors or outdoors.

The other players hide while a player known as the 'Seeker' closes their eyes in a designated spot and counts to 30. After the 'Seeker' counts to 30 they shout "ready or not here I come," and begins searching for the other hidden players. The last player to be found becomes the next 'Seeker'.

Hokey Pokey

The Hokey Pokey is best known as a song but it can also be a game for charges that have not grasped the concept of rules and teams.

The Hokey Pokey is for one or more players with a leader; that can be played indoors or outdoors.

Use the Hokey Pokey as an energy releasing activity. When in game play speed up each verse and the winner is whoever can still keep up with the words when the end of the song is reached.

Each time the verse is repeated replace what goes in and out starting with left arm, right arm, left leg, right leg, rear end, and whole self.

You put your left arm in.

You put your left arm out.

In, out, in, out.

Shake it all about.

You do the hokey pokey,

And you turn yourself around,

That's what it's all about.

    Woah, hokey pokey.

    Woah, hokey pokey.

    Woah, hokey pokey.

    Knees bent, arms stretched,

    Ra-ra-ra.

Hot and Cold

Hot and Cold is a two or more player game, best played indoors.

The players pick an object. One player becomes the 'Hunter' and leaves the designated playing area so they cannot hear or see the other players. The other players hide the object. Once the object is hidden the 'Hunter' is called back into the room and can immediately start looking for the object. The other players guide the 'Hunter' to the object by shouting "cool," "cold," "colder," and "ice cold" the further the 'Hunter' is from the object. As the 'Hunter' approaches the object the group will shout "warm," "warmer," "hot," and "burning hot," becoming hotter the closer the 'Hunter' is until the object is found. Then another object may be picked as another player becomes the 'Hunter'.

Red Light, Green Light

Red Light, Green Light is a two or more player game that can be played indoors or outdoors.

One player starts as the 'Traffic Light' whose job is to say "red light" or "green light". When the 'Traffic Light' shouts "green light" every player runs, walks, or dances until the 'Traffic Light' yells "Red Light" at which point all the players freeze in place, mid movement. If the 'Traffic Light' sees someone is still moving that player is out.

Simon Says

Simon Says is a two or more player game, best played in a large group, that can be played indoors or outdoors.

A player becomes 'Simon' and stands in front of all of the other players. 'Simon' shouts commands, using the phrase "Simon says" and the other players obey by performing the command. Players are out when they obey a command and 'Simon' didn't use the phrase, "Simon says."

- *Touch your toes.*
- *Touch your nose.*
- *Touch your knees.*
- *Spin around.*
- *Make a funny face.*
- *Stand on one foot.*
- *Sit down.*
- *Stand up.*
- *Put hands on hips.*
- *Reach for the sky.*
- *Wiggle like a worm.*

GOAL OF THE WEEK

There is always room for improvement. Set the tone for the week by selecting a new skill to learn or behavior to enhance. The goal doesn't have to be spoken or grand. If bathroom independence is the end goal, flushing the toilet may be the goal of the week. It is important not to force a charge but for charges to get there on their own with your guidance.

Goal of the week should be taken day by day. Enjoy the tiniest of wins. They all add up and get little ones to reach their next milestone.

HEALTH

Hand Washing

Hand washing is important to reduce transmitting contagious bacteria and viruses, improving health and reducing sick days for charges, nannies, and family members.

"Hand washing can prevent 1 in 3 diarrhea-related sicknesses and 1 in 5 respiratory infections, such as a cold or the flu." – Centers for Disease Control and Prevention (CDC). According to the London School of Hygiene and Tropical Medicine, hand washing with soap can save the lives of over 600,000 children every year.

When to Wash Hands

- *Before, during, and after preparing food.*
- *Before eating food.*
- *Before and after caring for someone who is sick.*
- *Before and after treating a cut or wound.*
- *After using the bathroom, changing diapers, or cleaning up a child who has used the bathroom.*

- *After blowing your nose, coughing, or sneezing.*
- *After touching an animal, animal food or treats, animal cages, or animal feces.*
- *After touching garbage.*
- *If hands are visibly dirty or greasy.*

How to Wash Hands

1. Wet hands with clean running water (warm or cold) and apply soap.
2. Lather hands by rubbing them together with the soap.
3. Scrub all surfaces of your hands, including the palms, backs, fingers, between your fingers, and under your nails. Keep scrubbing for at least 20 seconds. Need a timer? Hum the "Happy Birthday" song twice.
4. Rinse hands under clean running water.
5. Dry hands using a clean towel or air dry them.

CPR and First Aid

Obtaining CPR and First Aid certification is the industry standard for child caregivers and a crucial credential for most caregiver positions.

CPR and First Aid training increases safety, saves lives, relieves pain, and prevents situations from worsening. Depending on the course provider, certification lasts one to two years before it must be renewed by taking the training course again. There are numerous training course providers. The American Heart Association's website has a CPR and First Aid training locator to help people find the classes from every course provider nearest to them.

I HATE YOU

It comes in different forms, whether charges run when they see you or just tell you, "I hate you," but the feeling of being disliked by a charge is a hard one to get over. At its worst, the feeling of being hated by your charge can have fantastic nannies rethinking their position and wanting to quit. However, it is rare for a charge to truly hate their nanny. Growing up is tough and do not take it personally.

A charge's distaste for a nanny is generally not the nanny's fault. Dislike of a nanny can stem from anywhere. Replacing another nanny is an easy way to get on a child's bad side. Unfortunately, explaining the reasons their previous nanny is leaving hardly helps. Other times, enforcing the principal's rules, or your own, can be the wedge to make a charge think less than fondly of you. All is not lost, there are things every nanny can do to remedy the situation.

Agree

When a charge wants someone other than you, a family member or another nanny, talk about that person warmly. Listen and agree how wonderful that person is.

Once, in the middle of the night my 4-year-old charge woke up because he missed his sister who was away at camp. So, we wrote a letter to her.

I emailed it to his mom, who emailed it to his sister. He was thrilled the next morning. Not only did he receive a letter back from his sister but he also realized he wasn't alone when the rest of his family was talking about how much they missed her too.

Bond

Balance the daily struggles by connecting over something the charges truly love. Play a game of hide and seek, visit an ice cream parlor, or make a craft based on their favorite TV show. The key to bonding is doing an activity that requires little rules and structure so neither the nanny or charge, is in a power position. Think of bonding as relaxing together.

Treat Every Day as New

Give every day the chance for you and your charge to start over. Time will settle both a nanny and a charge's anxieties, but it takes an active nanny to try new things and experiment to turn the "I hate you" situation on its head. The saddest thing a nanny can do is accept that this is the way it is. A charge's harsh feelings can come up at any time. Charges often have a honeymoon period with a new nanny and only decide months later to start pushing back.

INDEPENDENCE

I actively use my role as a nanny to help charges achieve milestones, become independent and overcome daily obstacles.

Time

The pressure of needing to have something done right away is an independence crusher. It is important to avoid adding stress when children are acquiring a new skill and rigid time limits are more often than not the culprit. Create a relaxing environment for charges to succeed with an extra bumper of time on new skills. I usually add 10-15 minutes for new skills, like independently dressing.

Teaching

It seems mindless for adults, but learning a skill such as cleaning a table requires guidance and explanation. "We spray the cleaner into the towel and then rub it all over the surface of the table. We wipe the table with cleaner to remove bits of food and get rid of germs we can't even see to keep us from getting sick."

Encouragement

"You can do this," "I'm so proud of you," "just a little more," hugs and high fives go a long way in helping motivate children to take on a new skill that until this point they probably expected you to do for them. Motivation lets charges know you believe they are grown, able, and ready to take on zipping up their coats, buckling themselves in, and so much more. You might do such a good job with encouragement that you need to give yourself a pat on the back.

Practice

Leave the new skill up to the charge every time it needs to be completed. Doing it for them only gives children an escape on progressing and stifles their journey towards becoming independent.

Often, I meet capable and unchallenged children. Give charges a challenge, a chance, and let them achieve their new goal themselves. Independence is a state of mind. A child will leap at doing things for themselves once they know you believe in them.

INITIATIVE

The most sought-after nannies are the ones that are proactive and willing to take initiative. Taking initiative is taking control of a situation, assuming responsibility of its outcome and hoping the effort is appreciated. While it is appealing for principals to have a nanny on their team that is willing to put themselves out there, it is not something every nanny is initially comfortable doing. Initiative is a skill everyone is capable of learning.

Ways to Improve Initiative

- *Be Active.*

  No matter where you work there is always something to be done. Look around, if all your tasks are complete, then add some more. Wipe a table. Do an extra load of laundry. Clean a fish tank.

- *Learn New Skills.*

  If cooking isn't your strong suit, start practicing recipes. Make it fun and do it with your charge. Try your hand at sewing if a hem needs to be stitched up. Propel yourself forward by trying out new skills.

- *Speak Up.*

  Have you been thinking about taking your charges somewhere or signing the family up for a membership to a place the charges love because the family will save money if you do? Maybe you have a new plan to get the children to eat healthier foods or clean up after themselves. Your ideas are valued and principals want to hear from you. It doesn't matter what your ideas are, share them with the principals. The principals may get more jazzed about your ideas than you.

- *Better to Make a Decision than No Decision.*
  How do you know you made the right call? Everyone second guesses themselves. It is far better to make a choice than make no choice. Encourage yourself to make hard choices by recognizing you make plenty of great ones all the time.

- *Build Confidence by Starting Small.*
  Taking initiative and building confidence go hand in hand. Take a step forward by completing a task with a low or no risk for failure, like an extra load of laundry.

INTERVIEW

You want the position. Your cover letter and resume showed a family that you are cut above the rest. Now the family wants to know more. The interview is scheduled, now what?

Interviews are a chance to show off your accomplishments, special skills, and talk about yourself. Many people go into interviews a tad nervous but remember you are on equal footing. Interviews are a nanny's chance to determine if this family possess the qualities they are looking for in a family and work place too.

Where

There are often several interviews for nanny positions. Some start on the phone with a principal or agent and others begin on childcare websites when the first response from a posting is returned. These eventually lead to an in-home interview where the nanny is given the chance to meet the entire family and interact with the children. It is important to remain professional, well spoken, and thoughtful at every interaction when speaking with potential principals and agents. Think of each exchange as a mini interview, giving insight into who you are.

Attire

Dress to impress. Dressing professionally when interviewing for a position as a nanny means wearing business attire that is also comfortable. Wearing business attire shows that this meeting and position is important to you. Adorning a comfortable ensemble is also important for getting on the floor to play with the charges.

Bring

- *Printed cover letter, resume, letters of recommendation, and any relevant certificates such as a CPR and First Aid certification. Always bring enough copies for each principal attending to reference. Bring and hand out these documents every time you have an interview, even if it is the third time you've met with them.*
- *Note pad.*
- *Pen.*
- *List of thoughtful questions for the interviewer.*

Questions from the Family

The interviewer, either principals or agents, are looking to see if you are the right fit for the demands of this position and family. Some questions are more standard than others, for instance, "did you graduate high school or college?" Other questions will pertain specifically to the position you are applying for. A family may want to know if you are good at math if they recognize their child needs extra help in that subject. Be as specific as possible when answering.

There is no one correct answer to land a nanny position but answering honestly will save both you and the family time on the hunt for the right fit.

Standard Questions from the Family

- *What do you enjoy most about children?*
- *What is your background in childcare?*
- *How long have you been a nanny?*
- *What was your role as a nanny in other families?*
- *What ages of children have you cared for before?*
- *Do you smoke?*
- *Are you CPR and First Aid certified?*
- *Do you have a valid driver's license?*
- *Do you have your own car?*
- *Do you have any health problems?*
- *Can you swim?*
- *How do you feel about staying later on a moment's notice?*
- *Can you commit to a year or more with our family?*
- *What is your rate per hour?*
- *Why did you leave your last position?*

Questions for the Family

Having a few questions prepared for the family shows how professional and committed you are to this position. Prepared questions show that you put in more effort than merely showing up. Don't be surprised if you stump a family with a question. Other candidate may have never asked them questions before. Again, this is positively setting you apart.

Below are some general sample questions I ask families in an interview, but consider what you are looking for in a family and ask questions to see if they can accommodate your needs to thrive.

Standard Nanny Questions for the Family

- *Why are you looking for a nanny?*
- *What would be my responsibilities?*
- *Have you had a nanny in the past?*
- *If you have, why did the previous nanny leave?*
- *What qualities have you found to be lacking in other or previous nannies?*
- *Does your child (or children) have any medical conditions?*
- *Does this position come with any benefits (healthcare, PTO, parking)?*
- *How do you pay (check, cash, payroll service)?*
- *How long do you foresee needing a nanny?*
- *Is there anything you find difficult with your children that I may be able to address (picky eater, bed wetting, hitting)?*
- *How do you discipline your children?*

Red Flags

Childcare is very personal, differing from person to person and no family or position is like any other. Parents, more often than not, do not realize hiring a nanny makes them the CEO of a business, a business their nanny depends on. Some parents are better bosses than others. Before accepting a position make sure this family is the right fit for you and acknowledge any red flags you stumble across throughout the interview process.

- *Absent Principal or Child from the Interview.*
  Take notice if there is a family member, especially a child, you haven't met before accepting the position. Chances are the nanny will have to interact with everyone in the family at some

point and it is best to meet everyone before starting. As nanny you will be spending vast amounts of time with this charge. It is imperative that you and the child feel a connection, no matter how small.

- *Uncomfortable Talking about Money.*
Beware if a family is awkward confirming a salary or rate because that most likely means they are uncomfortable with the amount and this is money you will depend on receiving on time.

- *Cannot Commit to a Schedule or Start Date.*
Check why a family cannot confirm a start date. It may be a very reasonable reason, but it may be a sign they aren't certain they want your services and you are depending on this family for your income.

- *Disagree with the Parenting Choices.*
As a nanny for this family you will need to be able to respect and perhaps carry out their parenting style. If you notice an approach to childcare during the interview process that seems wildly different than how you care for children, it may be a sign that this position is not a good fit.

- *On the Spot Offer.*
If a family presents an on the spot offer, it could mean that they act without having a plan, think short sighted, or that they are desperate to fill the position.

- *The Interview is Actually a Babysitting Gig.*
An interview is for the nanny and family to get to know each other. Unfortunately, some nannies walk in to an interview only to have the parents say, "you're in charge and we will be back in a few hours." A nanny will usually babysit for the family

before the interview process is complete, but something might be wrong if babysitting is part of the first interview.

- *Disrespectful.*
  Whatever it may be, late, lack of eye contact, or distracted with their phone, acknowledge if you feel disrespected in the interview, when a family is trying to sell you on the position. It isn't going to get better when you officially work for them.

- *Looking for a Best Friend.*
  A family may lack professionalism if they say they are searching for a nanny that can also be a best friend or part of the family. It is great to have a strong connection, but once a nanny starts working, the labels of friends or family are often used against them. Nannies must be treated professionally to thrive.

Thank You Note

It is common to send a "thank you" note or email after an interview. Thank the interviewer for taking the time and effort to meet and get to know you to show that you are thrilled for the opportunity. Use the "thank you" as a last chance to stand out among the rest of the applicants.

J U N K   F O O D

Junk food can come in the form of a quick snack or an entire meal. If junk food is in the house it is most likely going to be consumed but that doesn't mean you have to give it to your charge. I want my charges to learn to pick the healthier choice. When it comes to cutting out junk food snacks, I like to give leading choices. I usually pack 3 bags each filled with a varying degree of healthy options. These examples are from my experience.

Bag 1) A food that my charges will not pick. ex. raisins.

Bag 2) A food they might pick. ex. vegetable chips.

Bag 3) A food I want them to try. ex. apples with the skin on.

It seems silly but children need to be introduced to food. Even being around new foods can be the spark to the healthier eating.

K

KNOWLEDGE

Knowledge is power. According to the 2017 International Nanny Association 'Salary-Benefits Survey' a nanny with more education or experience also means a higher hourly wage.

While experience as a nanny takes time on the job, advanced education, classes, and certifications can be attained at your own aspiring pace. Set your sites higher and pull away from the nanny and sitter competition by being a standout with specialty skills.

CPR, First Aid, and AED Certification

These three lifesaving certifications are the most important a nanny can get. Proof of CPR and First Aid training is a prerequisite for most nanny positions. All three certifications are usually taught in the same one time, three to four-hour class. Certification generally lasts for two years before it must be renewed.

Foreign Language Skills

For families that only speak one language but seek the educational advantage for children that know multiple languages, bilingual nannies are the cream of the crop. Bilingual nannies help progress learning a language through play and everyday interactions by offering charges constant exposure to another language and culture.

Driver's License

As running errands and drop-off and pick-ups have become increasingly inconvenient for principals, many families have turned to their nannies to pick up the slack. Nanny positions often require a spotless driving record and a valid driver's license to fulfill their family's driving needs.

Cooking Classes

Confidence in the kitchen requires no certification but if cooking isn't your thing, a culinary class may be the logical next step to round out your qualifications as a standout nanny. Many families desire a nanny with the skills to provide healthy meals for their children. Nannies that know their way around a kitchen are an asset for any family.

Crisis Intervention

Crisis intervention and prevention training instills people with confidence to properly respond with evidence-based strategies to identify and deescalate fears, anxiety, and hostile or violent behaviors before situations reach a boiling point. Crisis Intervention is a short-term counseling solution used by teachers, police officers, and sitters.

L

LAUNDRY BASICS

You've done your own laundry for years, but now is the time to make sure you're properly taking care of your employer's wardrobe.

Understanding the appropriate laundry settings to use on specific clothing will help maximize your schedule and determine the best time to put in the next load.

Laundry is deeply personal, so always ask how your employer prefers their laundry to be done. From separation, stain removers, and settings, your employer's preferences may surprise you.

Here are the basics.

The Washing Machine. Timing, Agitation, and Temperature.

Timing: The timer sets the amount of time clothing is in the machine. Longer for dirtier and heavier items while shorter for less unclean and delicate clothing. The less a garment is in the machine getting banged around, the longer it will last.

Agitation: The cycle is the force of the agitator against the clothing and it comes in two parts, "wash" and "spin." The wash cycle is when the detergent and water mix with the clothing and the cleaning is performed. The spin cycle is when the clothing is spun and rung out.

- *Regular = Fast wash & fast spin cycle.*
- *Permanent Press = Fast wash & slow spin cycle. This is best used on regular items that are prone to wrinkle.*
- *Delicate = Slow wash & spin cycle. This one says it all in its name, "delicate." This setting is for fine clothing that require a gentle touch.*

Temperature: Cold water is for darks. Hot water is for whites, brights, and heavily soiled items. When in doubt use cold water. Many years ago, detergents didn't dissolve as well in cold water and separating for temperature was much more important, but detergents have come a long way and many are able to dissolve in cold water. The cold-water setting is useful for conserving energy, and the life span of clothing. Hot water, over time, may induce fading.

Leaving the lid open when the washing machine isn't in use will prevent rusting, ensuring the machine to last its fullest.

Best Temperature to Wash Stains

- *Ball point pen ink: Warm or Hot*
- *Blood: Cold or Warm*
- *Chocolate or coffee: Warm or Hot*
- *Cosmetics: Warm or Hot*
- *Cream, Milk, Ice Cream: Warm or Hot*
- *Dirt, Mechanical/Cooking Oil: Warm or Hot*
- *Grape, Wine: Warm or Hot*

- *Grass: Warm or Hot*

- *Ketchup, Tomato Product: Warm or Hot*

- *Mud: Warm or Hot*

- *Perspiration: Warm or Hot*

- *Ring around the Collar: Warm or Hot*

Dryer Time and Temperature

Dryer settings have become increasingly specific. Heavy Duty, Duvet, Jeans, Knits, and Hand Dry tell the user exactly what type of items to use them for. However, there are dryer settings that never go out of style, Regular, Permanent Press, Delicate, Tumble Dry, and understanding them will take your next loads to the next level.

- *Regular is the highest heat setting the dryer is capable of. Best used for the heaviest and thickest items.*

- *Permanent Press is a medium heat with a cool down period to keep items as wrinkle free as possible. Best used on most apparel and especially items that wrinkle easily.*

- *Delicate is the lowest heat setting. Best used on delicate apparel and those that may be prone to shrinkage such as wools, cottons, and linen.*

- *Tumble Dry is the no heat option and most similar to hanging clothing on a line to dry. Best used for pieces that may shrink when heat is applied and for freshening garments up.*

Read the apparel's attached labels to learn how to best take care of all textiles.

Pilling

Pilling is small bits of fluff stuck to fabric. Pilling is usually caused when two fabrics rub against each other in the wash. To help eliminate pilling turn sweaters, workout clothes, and other tightly knit garments inside out before washing to reduce the amount of friction they have with each other in the wash. Don't waste your time with time household remedies to depill, do yourself a favor and use a depiller.

LISTS

Staying on task and accomplishing goals is nearly as simple as writing them all down. It is unmanageable to keep track of a mental to-do list for one, two, three, or more charges, principals, yourself and the family pets. Lists declutter lives into manageable steps.

Write Everything Down.

Write down everything that needs to get done on paper. This helps to sort items into the most important, quickest, and most immediate jobs to get done.

Break Down Tasks.

An unclear starting point will stop anyone in their tracks from getting things done. Take each task and break it down into little steps to give a road map for completion. A task road map is enormously important when teaching a charge how to use the potty, put on their clothes, or get ready for bed. Think of breaking down tasks as creating a recipe for to-dos. Breaking down a task can also lead to discovering short cuts and ways to improve how duties are accomplished.

Finish One Before Starting Another.

The Zeigarnik Effect shows that people remember their uncompleted tasks better and more detailed than ones they have finished. In short, putting projects off takes up brain power and impedes focus when moving onto the next project. However, if a project simply cannot be completed and you must move on, write down what is left for you to do before proceeding.

LISTENING

Listening goes both ways. Nannies and charges alike have to give it to get it.

Methods to Better Listening

- *One Instruction.*
  There may be a lot of information you would like to give to your charge but narrow it down to the actions they need to take. Giving too many instructions will surely lead to misunderstandings and incomplete tasks. Charges do not immediately need to know why they are leaving the park but they do need to know it is time to grab their belongings.

- *Step Away from Distractions.*
  At home or in public, pulling a charge aside and away from distraction is a great way for charges to focus and engage solely with you. Then you can make sure your charge understands the information you are giving them.

- *Try A Different Approach.*
  No one method to better listening will work 100% of the time. Switching up how, where, or when a charge is given information can make all the difference to enhance a charge's listening

skills. Different things work for different children. Some charges will respond better if they are always separated from distractions, even if it is just to tell them, "we are leaving in five minutes."

- *"Yes, If You Hear Me."*
  If your only trouble is getting a charge to acknowledge the information you've just given them, see *"Y" for "Yes, If You Hear Me."*

LYING

There is no doubt that lying is a problem. Lies stem from attention seeking, to avoid being in trouble, or to evade simple responsibilities like homework and chores. No matter the reason, regular lying can be a challenge to overcome. Bottomline, lying is unnecessary and a nanny's job is to help children understand that.

Nip Exaggerating in the Bud

Time after time I've seen a child's lie become an obstacle to getting what they truly want. I worked with a child that told tall tales to impress and get children to play with him on the playground, but it backfired and the others labeled him a liar. Children see the world in yes and no, right and wrong, black and white. Even though an adult can see it as exaggerating, a child's white lies might not play well to their peers that already know lying is wrong.

Steps to Overcome Lying

Over my tenure as a childcare provider I have seen my fair share of lying, and developed a simple way to get children back on track to telling the truth.

- *Give Charges Another Opportunity to Tell the Truth.*
  All is not lost when a charge lies. Give children a chance to correct their mistake. Lying isn't always done on purpose. "Is that what really happened?" is a fair question to ask any toddler if their story doesn't add up. Often a child will speak without thinking and giving them a second chance to clarify what they mean might be all it takes to get the truth.

- *Let Charges Know the Consequence of Lying.*
  A charge might think twice about proceeding with a lie if they are told what will happen if they aren't telling the truth. Sometimes a lie gets a charge a time out but other times a toy is taken away. Of course, the consequences depend on the lie and the situation.

- *Apologize.*
  All caregivers have been there, one tiny detail turns a whopper of a tale into a very plausible situation but by then we have already given a time out. Apologize as soon as you realize you have made a mistake.

- *Reward Charges with a Thank You When They Tell the Truth.*
  There is no doubt that lying is a problem. It is often shocking when children start lying regularly. Lying is unnecessary and it can create a ripple effect in their social lives. Furthermore, a charge's lies can set back our trust in them. Talk to children about why it is important to tell the truth. Thank charges for telling the truth because it may have been a challenge for them to do so.

M

MANNY

The need for a male nanny, aka a manny, is in growing demand. Over the years men have slowly been accepted into the child caregiver's community but still only make up 1% of it. Male nannies offer the same quality of care as female nannies but they can also be a positive male role model for families that may be in need of one. For single moms, two-mommy families, families whose father may travel and work long hours, or households where daughters outnumber a son, a positive male role model may help to shape girls' and boys' view of what a man can be.

A mother once told me, "I only want male nannies from now on. I think it is fantastic for my daughters and son to see a man cooking, cleaning, and supporting their emotional needs."

MAXIMIZE THE DAY

Everyone knows the early bird gets the worm because the early bird chose to maximize its day and get more done than the other birds thought was possible. Time is precious and it is impossible to get more.

Using the day to the fullest is tough but it is also empowering to check things off your list and move on to your next task. Maximizing the day is finding the under-utilized time to fit more things in.

- *Create a Routine for Efficiency.*

  So much time is wasted deciding what to do next. Routines create efficiency by taking away the day's guesswork and planning what task or activity is to come next.

- *Have a Plan for the Next Day.*

  Whether it is written down or kept mentally, a plan for the next day will keep you from stumbling around, wasting time, and leaving responsibilities unfulfilled. Before bed or during a spare moment, list what needs to be accomplished the next day and how and when those tasks can be achieved.

- *80/20 Rule, the Pareto Principal.*

  Named after its inventor, Vilfredo Pareto, the Pareto Principal, aka the 80/20 rule, states that 2 out of 10 tasks are worth more than the rest combined. People spend 80% of their time working on endeavors that will contribute very little to their overall success. Accomplish more by utilizing the Pareto Principal. Take out a piece of paper and write down ten things you need to do, then circle the two items that will provide the most value. Of those top two most valuable items, do the harder one first.

- *Me Time.*

  People over invest themselves in their work only to flounder, disengage and become burnt out. There are many reasons employees withdraw but devoting time for themselves can reenergize and reconnect them with the joys of their profession. Having "me time" isn't easy. Often when people pull back their devotion to work, they feel a void and become restless or uninspired. Learning what you truly desire takes time and will likely take trying many things. Be open to alone time, time with friends, and adventures. Give yourself a chance to recharge, because if you're feeling overwhelmed or uninterested in your work position you are languishing and missing the joy that brought you to the nanny profession in the first place.

M O O D

It is normal to go through bouts of struggles. Nannying is a bit like being the captain of a ship. Some days are clear and bright while others are stormy and rough. If things seem out of whack for you and your charge, stand back and try to look at the bigger picture of what is going on in your and their lives? Children are great at picking up on moods. Do your best to leave your troubles at the door and enter with a big smile so they pick up on a great one.

NANNY VS. OTHER CHILD CAREGIVERS

People often confuse the many caregiver positions a family may have. Below are the most common.

Nanny

A nanny is a fully invested childcare provider and employed by a family. Nannies are usually responsible for charges and other duties to best serve the home. Nannies are employed by a family at part time (less than 30 hours/week) or full time (30+ hours/week). Some positions are "live-in" which means living accommodations, such as a room or a coach house are provided. Nanny shares are when a nanny cares for children of two or more families.

Au Pair

An au pair is a person ranging from about 18-26 years old and enrolled in a government authorized cultural exchange program where they exchange living arrangements with a family, in a foreign country, for childcare or other domestic services. Au pairs working in the U.S. must receive a minimum of $195/week as stated in the Fair Labor Standards Act.

Babysitter

A babysitter is only employed for a few hours to look after children on behalf of their principals. Babysitters are often referred to as a "sitter" because they look after children of various ages.

Family Assistant

A family assistant is a family's personal assistant. Family assistants are able to step in wherever the principals need them, whether that be running errands all day or childcare.

House Manager

A house manager is an administrative position overseeing and training a family's domestic staff, vendors, and contractors. House managers responsibilities vary in every home but their function is to make sure the household is maintained and running smoothly. Tasks may include cleaning, ordering/buying, hiring vendors, and pet care.

NEGOTIATING

One of the many slippery slopes in taking care of children is negotiating with charges, but it isn't wrong. The problem is that over time it can lead caregivers or principals to inadvertently hand over nearly all their power in too many situations. Negotiating lets charges believe that they make the rules or that rules sometimes do not apply. Tantrums may arise when a child expects to get their way but can't because you are trying to take back control.

There is a time and a place for negotiating with charges. No one likes being told what to do and it is especially hard for children because they are constantly being told what to do.

When is negotiating ok? Put limits and boundaries on choices. Give two choices opposed to everything being available. Instead of asking, "what would you like for snack?" Ask, "would you like blueberries or apple slices for snack?" Give children the power for when and where it is appropriate for their family and nanny.

NOTES

Note Pad

Always bring a notepad to work and be ready to use it. Note taking is advantageous to nannies because it creates a record of the information that was either given to or generated by the nanny to ensure details don't fall through the cracks. It may be convenient to take notes on a cellphone but it can also seem disrespectful when doing it in front of a principal. A notepad conveys focus, engagement, and attention to detail while phones are analogous to distraction. If you prefer to keep notes on a smart phone write information down on a notepad and transfer it to a phone later.

Message Board

Principals and nannies' time are valuable and a message board is an easy way to solve the sometimes-complex problem of finding a moment to touch base to ask a question, or provide an answer.

ORGANIZATION

Organization is having items placed in a logical order or area, and organizing a home is not easy for everyone.

There are numerous benefits to an orderly home.

- *Save money by not repurchasing and using items already owned.*
- *Save time by reducing the search for belongings and knowing where items are kept.*
- *Reduce lost and misplaced belongings when items have a known storage place.*
- *Create an appealing and inviting living space.*
- *Prolong cleanliness and keep messiness at bay.*

Display, Instead of Hide, Meaningful Items.

Many times, people's key to cleaning is dumping items in a tub never to be seen again. Unfortunately tossing a mess away only creates the impression of order without providing it. Best case scenario is to find places for items to be stored neatly. Use a clear container when belongings must be contained so they are easily found. This is extremely useful in the kitchen, as people won't eat what they can't see.

Clean Living.

Cleanliness is created by habit. Continually take the time to treat yourself to a sparkling home by always putting items back where they belong.

Accept Some Clutter.

Some mess is in order. A toy box is never going to be organized. It is pointless for some continually used, everyday items (toys, pens, etc.), to be kept as if they are on display at a museum. Instead these everyday items are best kept in eye pleasing containers and purposeful spots. Everyone has a junk drawer; the key is to make sure there is only one per home. Pro tip: throw away pens that do not work right away.

Reachability is King.

Store the most commonly used items so they are easily accessible. There is no point keeping a pot or pan in a hard to reach place or in a place that is a chore to find and get.

Reachability is King for Children.

Children shouldn't need to ask an adult to help them get something they use all the time. Keep charge's clothes and belongings in easy to reach places that need minimal organizing so they can find things without the aid of an adult. When it comes to kids in the kitchen, find a drawer or cabinet to keep the charge's dinnerware so they can get cups, plates, bowls, and utensils for themselves.

ORIENTATION

Like every work place, a little orientation is necessary to get up to speed. For nannies, orientation is needed within the home and the surrounding neighborhood. Inside the home, orientation is becoming familiar with where everything you and your charges need is stored. Every household is different and everyday items are stored in different places.

Things to Identify the First Day Inside the Home

- *First Aid Kit*
- *Dinnerware*
- *Cookware*
- *Dishwasher*
- *Washer/Dryer*
- *Children's rooms*
- *Any area children and/or nanny are not allowed*

Things to Identify the First Day Outside the Home

- *Children's schools*
- *Fed Ex/UPS*
- *Indoor play spaces*
- *Lesson locations*
- *Memberships (athletic clubs, museums, play spaces, zoo)*
- *Playgrounds*
- *Preferred convenience stores (Target, Walmart, Walgreens, etc.)*
- *Preferred grocery stores (Alberts, Kroger, Waitrose, Whole Foods)*

OVERNIGHTS

Many nannies stay overnight from time to time while the principals are away. It can seem that there is very little difference when staying for the night but it is always good to go over possible extra responsibilities (bath time, bed time, meal time, medications, & walking pets) and compensation.

Speak up when it comes to payment with what you are comfortable receiving for staying overnight and performing extra responsibilities. Standard compensation for staying overnight is the nanny's usual hourly rate until the charge is asleep plus a flat rate of $75-$150 to when the charge wakes up.

P

PEE ON THE TOILET SEAT

If the little boy you watch enjoys standing up when he urinates, chances are he pees on the seat and floor. Unlike with adult men, we can't be that upset that little boys leave some poorly aimed pee on the seat. Where an adult man should have the wherewithal to lift up the seat before he uses it and cleans up when he's finished, little boys often cannot reach to put the seat up before they use the toilet.

If pee lands on the toilet seat, show and encourage your charge to rip off a piece of toilet paper, wipe the urine, toss the toilet paper in the toilet, and flush. Then, like every time, he should wash his hands. Feel free to teach this to any man who also leaves pee on the seat.

PICKY EATERS

Changing a picky eater's habits may be one of the toughest jobs there is. However, it isn't necessarily the nanny's job to change a charge's eating habits, though some principals might love it if you try.

- *Get Principals on Board.*

  Children learn a lot from the adults they are around, including eating habits. If the principals are picky eaters then you may be dead in the water. If the principals would like to see their little ones eat a wider variety of food then they also need to commit to changing their child's eating habits just as much as the nanny.

- *Respect.*

  Changing a picky eater's eating habits starts with teaching table manners and replacing "I don't like that," with a respectful, "no thank you." Don't get discouraged with a charge's outrageous and age appropriate reactions. The younger a charge, the more visceral their emotions come out. Set up boundaries to keep things civilized. When a child tosses food on the floor let them know that reaction isn't polite.

- *Stop Snacking.*

  Children fill up easily and don't need a lot of food to get through the day. A picky eater will have no problem skipping a meal if they had a snack, no matter how small, or if they know a snack is waiting around the corner.

- *Desserts are a Reward.*

  Desserts are a treat and should only be given when a charge finishes everything on their plate. This sets the expectation for a charge to finish their food. This should be consistent with every meal whether they are trying a new food on their plate or an old favorite.

- *Be Diverse.*

  Like a disk jockey plays a mix of classic hits and new tunes, make some days about challenging a charge to expand their palette and other days give them their favorite meals.

- *Portion.*

  Have new foods take up more space on the plate or serve them first. Charges that can get full on the foods they enjoy will never try anything new.

- *Reward.*

  Give a reward during dessert when a charge tries something new, I give an extra cookie. Start by rewarding a charge at dessert after they take one bite of a new food. Then at a different meal of the same food, move the goal post to giving the reward when they finish the entire portion.

- *Time Limits.*

  The best thing I ever did at meal time to help my picky eaters try new foods was add a time limit. Charges sit at the table until meal time is over or their plate is completely clean, getting every chance to clean their plate and earn dessert. However, if charges clean their plate before meal time is over, they now have extra play time. Even five minutes of extra play can be a major motivation.

- *Distractions.*

  Children will often distract themselves at the table to avoid trying something new. Eliminate distractions by no longer allowing toys at the table. If a charge is distracting themselves by constantly engaging with you at the table, finish your meal and then excuse yourself. Circle back to check on their progress.

- *Unorthodox.*

  Children's taste buds are a thing of their own. If a charge loves ketchup and will only eat apple slices with ketchup on it, let them. The most important part is getting a charge to try new foods. Skip the judgement and praise the success of trying.

- *One Bite Rule.*

   The one bite rule is setting the standard that a child has to try or they will never know if they like something or not. Say, "it is ok not to like something, but we have to try."

PLAYDATES

Playdates are essential for nurturing a charge's social awareness and development. While being an overall wonderful way for charges and nannies to spend some time with others, playdates are a surefire way for nannies to gain peers and flourish professional relationships in an otherwise peerless occupation.

Playdates are not free babysitting. Most nanny contracts include a clause stipulating that playdates are a possibility and nannies will be responsible for their charge and their playdate plus one without additional compensation. Speak to the principals to understand what is expected of you before taking on a playdate arranged by them. Nannies will need to have some upfront information about a visiting playmate; including dietary restrictions or preferences, if they have allergies, and fears that should be made aware to the nanny. Many principals encourage their nanny to set up playdates themselves.

Do not drop off charges and come back to pick them up. Nannies must stay when they and their charge are guests. Similarly, nannies that are hosting a playdate should expect the visiting child's guardian to stick around. However, if the playdate's guardian must leave, and you have okayed it, make sure to have their phone number, an emergency phone number, and a time to expect them back for pick up.

POLITE

Young charges often have zero tact because they don't know any better. Children can be demanding. When charges say they want things "now" and "faster" try asking, "can you please say that nicer?"

When charges don't know how to say something politely, demonstrate to them the way you would like to hear them ask for something. Then have them try asking again. It might not sound perfect but it is a step in the right direction.

Courtesy never goes out of style. Though you might feel like a broken record, you can't go wrong reminding your charges to say "please" and "thank you".

POTTY TRAINING READY?

Many principals hire nannies for their expert childrearing guidance. Often principals seek nannies who have potty trained children before. There are many methods on how to train charges to use the toilet and you may want to try several of them. Some nannies make a day of it and have their charge sit on the potty every 20 minutes hoping that will coax them to use it. Potty training is a process that takes courage, nerve, and more than a day. Potty training can feel like two steps forward and one step back. While writing this section, my mother reminded me of the adage, "no one walks down the aisle wearing a diaper."

Signs a Child is Ready to Potty Train.

- *Expresses a curiosity in using the bathroom.*

- *Predictably urinates and/or has a bowel movement.*

- *Able to stay dry for several hours.*

PREPARE

Assemble a "go bag" to take with whenever leaving the home. A "go bag" can be a backpack or tote bag and does not have to be fancy. "Go bags" should be packed with everything a nanny and charge need while on an adventure of any size.

- *Luggage tag, in case it is misplaced.*
- *First Aid Kit*
- *Medication*
- *Change of clothes, for the charge & maybe for the nanny.*
- *Wipes*
- *Snack*
- *Water bottles*
- *Toy, or game, or puzzle, or etc.*
- *Membership passes to frequented places.*

PRINCIPAL / PRIN·CI·PAL / 'PRINS'P'L/ ADJECTIVE

1. First in order of importance; main.
2. The industry term for a parent and/or guardian.

PROACTIVE

Proactivity is both anticipating people's needs and seeking to get what you need. The nanny must be proactive and speak to the principals whenever they have questions or concerns. It happens far too often, that a nanny will keep their true feelings hidden from the principals and build resentment over what is usually a misunderstanding. Speaking up is important and the only way to get what you need, be it understanding, a raise, or an answer to a question.

Speaking up should be done in person, with great tact, and at a good time for both the principals and yourself. Avoid sending an email or a text if the topic has been weighing on your heart or is about money, because texts and email can be easily misinterpreted. Do not put off topics that weigh on your heart. If there never seems to be a good time, tell the principals that you have a few questions or concerns and ask if there is a time that would be good to discuss them.

Nannies should never reply, "ok," if they do not truly understand or agree with what a principal is asking them to do. The easiest way to gain clarification and avoid a misunderstanding is to reiterate, in your own words, back to the principals what they just said. If you disagree with a direction from a principal immediately share your concern.

Speaking up and being proactive to get answers and clarification is the courteous thing to do. It far outweighs feeling miserable over what may be a miscommunication. Trust that the principals want what is best for you and their children.

POSITIONS

There are many opportunities to become a nanny. Families need nanny services ranging from several hours once a week to living with a family; some families even require two nannies. No matter the opportunity, each position can be broken down into four categories.

Responsibilities: The daily tasks that must be completed.

Nannies have a wide variety of responsibilities depending on the household. When writing a resume, applying, and interviewing be sure to keep in mind and address the places you shine.

Responsibilities may include: Newborn care. Sleep training. Reaching developmental milestones. Dishwashing. Washing and folding laundry. Providing age appropriate games, crafts, activities, and outings. Assisting with homework and studying. Cooking meals for children and/or families. Packing for trips, arranging travel accommodations and logistics. Grocery shopping and ensuring that the pantry/refrigerator is properly stocked.

Qualifications: The experiences that makes a nanny a good fit.

Qualifications are the standards of excellence and abilities a nanny possesses. Personality weighs just as much as experiences when it comes to clicking with principals and charges.

Qualifications may include: Experience with newborns. Passionate about child development. Ability to travel domestic and internationally. Ability to take direction. Ability to maintain discretion. Willingness to take initiative. Positive attitude. Calm in stressful situations. Flexible schedule. Creative. Musical. Active.

Requirements: The essential checklist of accomplishments and commitment needed.

Every family's needs are different. Background and expertise in certain areas may be what sets one nanny apart from the rest.

Requirements may include: High school or GED diploma/certificate. College degree. Verifiable professional experience working with specific ages of children. Verifiable one to five years full time nanny experience. Two to four professional references. Driver's license. Clean driving record. Non-smoker. Ability to pass a background check. CPR and First Aid certification. Up to date vaccinations. One to five year commitment to a family.

Compensation: The benefits an employee receives in exchange for services.

Compensation can vary drastically depending on the area, commitment, tasks, and knowledge a nanny may require. Starting at minimum wage and ranging to $100,000 annual salary and up. While some nanny positions are similar to babysitting, others are like being the chief care officer for a family; with the benefits to back it up.

Compensation and benefits may be: Paid time off. Furnished apartment/condo provided. Health insurance. Gym membership.

QUESTIONS

Always have a follow up question when a principal gives a task. Some people have little to no clue how specific they want projects done or items bought until projects are done differently or a brand other than what they are used to is purchased. When asked to retrieve an item from the grocery store ask for the preferred brand. If the principal wants a charge to get a haircut ask what style? Asking a follow-up and "just making sure" question will be very much appreciated and soon become second nature.

QUALITY TIME

Undivided attention and interacting are the ways to a charge's heart. Getting to know a charge means getting on the floor and discovering what they are interested in. Bonding is running around the playground with them instead of watching from the bench.

Quality time is sharing your passions, bringing them into your world, and taking part in their interests. Quality time is doing that one thing your charge always asks you to do but you never have time for. Take a moment, even when you are under a time crunch, to just play with your charge however they want. Having a charge join you in the kitchen to help make lunch or just make a s'more is also time well spent and gives them insight to your duties.

RESUME AND COVER LETTER

Resume

Writing a resume can be intimidating, even more so if this is your first resume and you are unsure if you have any previous positions to list. A resume is a snap shot of a person's most relevant work, education, skills and accomplishment history for the position they are seeking.

- *Customize.*

  Each job submission deserves its own tailored resume. This document is a snapshot of you and making it unique shows your dedication. It may only be a few changes here or there but having a resume specific to this position will set you apart from the other applicants.

- *Contact Information.*

  Use your name as the header and list your contact information below it (address, email, phone).

- *Easy to Read.*

  Employers sort through many applications for a single position so they need to be able to understand it at a glance. Use an easy to read font: Georgia, Helvetica, Veranda, etc.

- *Create Clear Sections.*

  Contact information, employment, education, skills, accomplishments.

- *Leave White Space.*

  Don't crowd the document with too much, making it overwhelming.

- *Use Reverse Chronological Order.*

  List work, education, and etc. history from most recent, at the top, to oldest, at the bottom.

- *One Page.*

  Limit a resume to one page. Employers aren't going to look at a second page nor should they have to. Cut it down to the most important and relevant information to that position.

- *Proofread.*

  It is impossible to proofread a resume too much. Have others read it. Read it out loud to yourself. Make sure it reads clearly and how you intend it to read. Use spell check and confirm grammar. Be sure to catch all the mistakes before it goes out.

- *Save as PDF when Sending.*

  Clearly label the PDF as your resume (Smith Nanny Resume 2020) and save it as a PDF if you are sending it through email.

- *Examples.*

  There is no one way to create a resume. Search the internet for examples and guidance.

Cover Letter

A cover letter is absolutely vital and is just as important as a resume. However, many people believe cover letters are optional and skip them.

Think of a resume as a movie's end credits and the cover letter as the movie. The cover letter is a snap shot of you but a more complete picture to support and give a resume context. A cover letter should tell a little about yourself and why that makes you the perfect candidate for this position.

- *Uniform.*

  Make sure the resume and cover letter match. Keep the header and contact information in the same place and use the same font.

- *Customize.*

  Tailor a cover letter to the specific position you are applying for. Use the cover letter to your advantage by referencing skills, accomplishments, previous positions and how they pertain to items listed in the job description.

- *Forget "To Whom It May Concern".*

  A cover letter is a letter and it must be addressed to a specific individual, family or "Hiring Manager of XYZ Agency" instead of "To Whom It May Concern."

The resume's sections Easy to Read, One Page, Proofread, Save as PDF, and Examples all equally apply to cover letters.

REWARDS

The yin to discipline's yang is rewards. Just like loss of privileges acknowledges bad behavior, rewards acknowledge good behavior. Rewards of any sort, kind words, treats, or pats on the back, are needed to curb unwanted behavior by rewarding a charge's positive actions. Keep an eye out for wonderful behavior and reward it because charges don't instinctively know when they are doing something positive unless they are recognized for it.

REWARD CHART

Reward charts are all around us. Just think of the points program for a credit card or a "buy ten, get one free" card you find at your favorite car wash. Whatever the task or behavior, getting a charge to do something new is no cakewalk. Different things work for different children and at different ages, but a reward chart is a great start to letting children know that certain behaviors or tasks are favorable.

I have used reward charts to encourage listening, putting belongings away, and getting ready to leave the home faster. I have also used the charts to reduce potty accidents and to encourage charges to go to the bathroom. No matter the problem, a reward chart is a good first go to.

Reward Charts are fast, easy, and cheap to create. Adding check marks to a blank piece of paper will do the trick.

Problem. Solution. Reward.

1. Make sure to introduce the chart by letting the children know the issue why it was created. "I see you have a hard time putting your toys away when you are done using them."

2. Address the chart's function. "You will get a sticker every time you put your toys away."

3. What reward the charge will get in return to encourage the process. "After you get 25 stickers, which means putting away your toys 25 times, you will get a cookie."

Make sure the children know the reward (cookie, field trip, playdate, etc.) at the beginning to help them picture why they are working so hard. Rewards do not have to be fancy. I opt for dessert treats because they are inexpensive and gone once they are eaten. If a charge cannot read make sure to incorporate pictures.

RIGHTS

As employees, nannies are protected with basic workplace rights set in place by state and federal labor laws, tax laws, and penal code. All employees providing a service to a family, regardless if a nanny is a U.S. citizen or an alien with or without a work permit, are guaranteed protection.

Pay for Hours Worked

The Federal Fair Labor Standards Act states nannies are to be paid for all hours worked.

Wage

- *Regular Payments.*
  Payroll dates are to be regulated as weekly, bi weekly, semi-monthly, and monthly. Each state has its own rule but paydays are no less than once a month in all 50 states.

- *Minimum Pay.*
  The federal government set minimum wage to $7.25/hour in July of 2009 in accordance with the Fair Labor Standards Act. However, many states have set minimum wages higher than the federal government's standard. Nannies are to be paid the greater sum of either the federal or state's mandate.

- *Overtime Pay.*
  Live out nannies are entitled to overtime pay, 1.5 times the nanny's typical hourly rate, when working surpasses 40 hours per week. However, California, Hawaii, Maryland, and New York's labor laws have included this overtime pay for live-in nannies as well.

- *Loss Wages Due to Workplace Injury.*

  Workers' Compensation is an insurance policy taken out by the principals to cover the cost of loss wage and medical bills of employees who have suffered a work-related injury or illness. Workers' Compensation is afforded to nannies and regulated differently in each state. Most commonly employees must file a state workers' compensation claim. However, principals without workers' compensation insurance are generally liable for a nanny's benefits determined by the state.

- *Documentation.*

  Nannies are entitled to copies of any signed employment agreement and contracts. Passports, work permits, social security cards, driver's license, or any other identification document may not be kept from nannies. Principals must also keep accurate payroll records documenting dates and hours worked, for at least 3 years.

- *Retaliation.*

  Homeland Security's Immigration and Customs Enforcement Agency policies specify that employers cannot retaliate against employees for formal or informal workplace complaints, about unpaid wages, criminal conduct, etc., by turning them into authorities for immigration violations.

ROUTINES

Whether you realize it or not everyone uses routines everyday to help it move along smoothly. Routines and schedules alike take the guesswork and anxiety out of what lies ahead.

I have created routines to help charges clean up, face fears, eat a wider variety of foods, sleep train, and deal with anger. Creating and developing a routine by adding steps and setting boundaries can ease many of the daily problems a charge faces.

Routine Clean Up

Changing a charge's mindset to believe cleaning is cool can be a monumental task but a worthwhile challenge. Of course, children come into the world with someone doing everything for them and they are not going to give that up easily. However, children love being a part of the action and the nudge of handing them a spray bottle might be all they need to begin their journey to becoming a perfectionist.

- *Announce Time Remaining.*
  Letting children know 5-10 minutes before an activity change lets them get the most out of whatever they are doing and mentally prepare themselves for what is to come next.

- *Give Children Time.*
  Allow plenty of time for charges to put their belongings away because they aren't going to be fast.

- *Keep Yourself in Check.*
  Do your best to keep cleaning up from being urgent. Making clean up pressing is just shooting yourself in the foot. The harder it is to do something the less anyone wants to do it. If you are becoming stressed out or find you are adding stress to the process it is in your best interest to leave the room and let your charges give it a go alone.

- *Remind Charges It Is Clean Up Time.*
  It takes some reminding to keep clean up time from shifting back to extra free play.

- *Reward.*

  Woo hoo! The charges cleaned up. It is time to show how proud of them you are. The space isn't going to be perfectly put back together but getting charges to clean up is a big step at any age.

Routine Nap Time or Bed Time

- *Announce Time Remaining.*

  Inform your charges that nap time or bed time is in 5-10 minutes. The 5-10-minute warning lets charges get the most out of whatever they are doing and prepare themselves for what is to come next.

- *Relax.*

  Reading is a wonderful transition activity for sleeping. Read in a calm voice or whisper and let the tone of your voice set the mood to relax.

- *Countdown to Lights Off.*

  Keep charges from fussing around in the dark with a 10 second countdown to get comfy in bed while standing at the light switch. When the 10 seconds are up and the lights are off they have mentally told themselves they are cozy.

- *Leave the Room.*

  It is ok to stay in the room for a bit to ease a charge's mind. Constantly try different approaches to nap/bedtime if you find yourself lingering in the room at the request of the child. I have discovered staying in the room kept my charges up longer than if I just wished them a good nap time and stepped out.

  If a child is attempting a conversation with you swiftly shut it down. Focus them on sleep by reminding them it is time to go to bed and to save the talking for later. Remind them that you will have to leave the room if they keep talking because it is distracting them from going to sleep. Stay true to your word if a charge continues to talk by wishing them a good nap or bed-time and step out.

Routine Toys/Belongings Left Out

It is inevitable that charges and principals play while nanny is away. Since nanny isn't there to put things back, most families leave out more items over the weekend than they normally would during the week. While it is often part of the job, it can be frustrating to put back mounds of toys. I developed a routine to teach my charges to put their most beloved belongings away.

- *Gather All Toys/Items Left Out.*
  It may be one item or it may be a towering stack. Pick out a place, a table or in a bin, and place the left out toys there.

- *Show Charges All the Items They Left Out.*
  Reveal the collection of left out items to the charges. Make sure the charges have time to deal with this problem and put their items back. Showing charges a collection of their belong-ings before school when they cannot do anything to get them back will not help and may only cause distraction or esca-late behaviors.

- *Give a Chore.*
  Give charges a chore to complete before they are allowed to begin putting their belongings away. Chores give a sense of responsibility. The chores do not have to be hard. You will discover there are chores for nearly any age. Wiping a table, sweeping, folding napkins, or making the beds will do the trick. Chores can even be fun with the help of a spray bottle.

There is no rule that charges have to do the chore themselves either, nannies can definitely help.

- *Belongings Go Back Before They Are Used Again.*
  Have charges put their toys and other belongings back before playing with them again. Putting their items back reminds charges where their things go. Some toys probably never had a specific place to go and is why there were left out. I often reiterate, "if you do not know where they belong, ask me and we can find the perfect place for them together."

SCHEDULE

Children and nannies alike want to know what is happening, when it is going to happen, where the happening is at, and they should be able to get those answers.

Replacing chaos with predictability will change a family's life for the better. A perfected schedule can take away the stress of trying to fit everything in to the time you're scheduled for that day. Creating a schedule will develop and evolve over time as you figure out how to fit tasks in and become more efficient to get chores done.

Charges are going to act out when a wrench is thrown into their routine. I can always tell when a charge didn't go to bed on time. Stay on top of what is to come next because it is going to affect them and you.

Not everyone likes surprises. Some surprises go too far and give children anxiety. Let charges know if the day's pace is going to differ from what they are used to so they can be prepared. If the day is going to be different tell the charge that they are going to do something extra fun, then let the details of the event be the surprise.

Schedule Example

6:30 AM
- Wash and put away dishes.
- Prepare breakfast.
- Clean tables.
- Put away minor messes.

7:30 AM
- Wake up charges.
- Help charges get dressed.
- Potty, brush teeth, etc.
- Help charges make beds.
- Charges eat breakfast.

8:10 AM
- Bus dishes from breakfast.
- Get ready for school (jackets, shoes, bags).
- Head to car/buckled into car seats.
- Principle drives them to school.

8:20 AM
- Wash final dishes (from breakfast).
- Turn on dish washer.

8:30 AM
- Break.

11:30 AM
- Pick up three-year-old from school.
- Arrive home,
- Three-year-old bathroom break.
- Prepare lunch.

12:00 PM
- Lunch
- Three-year-old grabs napkin, utensils, dishes.

1:00 PM

- Put lunch away.
- Quiet time (read, draw, low key play, chores).
- Check upstairs and downstairs for cleaning.
- Start laundry.
- Go to the park.
- Errands.

2:30 PM

- Three-year-old potty break.
- Head to car/buckled into car seat.

2:40 PM

- Leave to pick up five-year-old (watch out for long trains).

3:00 PM

- Five-year-old pick up.

3:20 PM

- Arrive home.
- Charges potty break.
- Play time (go to the park, craft, build with Legos).
- Get nanny tasks complete (laundry).

5:10 PM

- Start dinner while charges play.

5:30 PM

- Dinner.
- Post dinner chores (wash dishes, wipe down table and island).

7:00 PM

- Play time.

7:35 PM

- Clean up.

7:45 PM

- Bath time.
- Three-year-old potty break/takes a bath while five-year-old flosses/brushes teeth.
- Then switch.
- Five-year-old put in retainers.
- Bed time, pick out books, and put on PJs.

8:30 PM
- Read one book each then lights off.
- Bed time.

SCREEN TIME

Rules for screen time differ family to family. While the science is being worked out it is best to keep screen time in moderation. Ask the principals for their views and how they would like you to handle screens. If possible, screen time is best left for principals who have worked all day to give as a treat to their children after the nanny has gone home.

SOCIAL MEDIA

We live in a world where sharing what you are doing at any giving moment is more than acceptable, it is encouraged. However, on the job, it is imperative a nanny keep information about their employer and position confidential. Nanny employment contracts often forbid posting photos or referencing charges or employers on any social media platform. These are simply not our lives or children to share with on social media. However, if the need is that great, it is acceptable to ask the principal how they feel about you posting a photo or moment you are dying to share.

Many sites and forums for nannies and sitters are monitored by agencies and families so be careful what you share. If you aren't comfortable asking, don't feel comfortable posting.

SICK

Sick Children

Watching a sick charge can be nerve wracking, intimidating, and a little shocking. Seeing a child that is normally extremely active, stuck in bed is unsettling and can have any nanny questioning their childcare abilities. Sick days may also include extra responsibilities, such as giving medications and additional cleaning. Then there are questions like, "are they contagious," and, "will I get sick?" A nanny should be proactive when taking care of a sick charge and wash their hands a lot.

Before a charge becomes sick, nannies and principals should have a discussion to weigh the pros and cons of nannies taking care of a sick charge because nannies may get sick and need to use sick days.

- *Critical Decisions.*
  It is important to take the weight off the nanny's shoulders of making critical decisions for a sick charge by asking what the principals would like the nanny to do in multiple situations.
  - Is there any circumstance for the nanny to contact the principals?
  - When should "as needed" medication be given?
- *Contacting Principals.*
  Nannies should instantly contact the principal whenever they are unsure of what to do. Taking care of a sick charge can throw the best nannies for a loop. It is vital not to feel embarrassed about not knowing what to do next and move forward to get the charge the care they need.

- *Medication Chart.*

Write a list to keep track of everything being done and given to a sick charge. Indicate what medication, the time it was given, and how much was given to the charge, as well keeping track of the charge's temperatures if the child has flu like symptoms. It is impossible to be too thorough.

Sick Nanny

A sick nanny is always a challenge for a family because there usually isn't another person who can easily step in to perform the nanny's duties. However, nannies are human too and sick days are inevitable. The best way to deal with nanny's sick days is for the principals and nanny to agree on a "Nanny Sick Day Plan" long before they need to take one.

A barebones "Nanny Sick Day Plan" will consist of what or who is the backup childcare and how much notice the nanny will need to provide the family.

- Give principals as much time as possible to put their back up plan into action.

- Decide if sick days are paid. Part of your "Nanny Sick Day Plan" will be determining if sick days are paid or not. The International Nanny Association determined only 67% of nannies have paid sick days. Sick day pay is different for each family because principals may have to pay someone else to take care of their child. Deciding on what is fair before a contract is signed will put everyone's mind at ease.

- Nannies must only use sick days when they are actually sick.

SLEEP AND NAPS

There are numerous tips and tricks to getting children to sleep and you will find that everyone under the sun is willing to give you their advice.

Being consistent and creating a bed or nap time routine, such as dimming the lights and story time, is imperative for charges to get the most out of their sleep. A cool temperature in a quiet room is the best environment to promote a healthy sleep hygiene.

Newborns seem to be randomly awake or asleep because they have not developed their sleep/awake cycles, which fully develop at around 6 months for most babies.

Putting a drowsy baby or child in their crib or bed before they fall asleep will help to teach them how to soothe themselves to sleep. Children that fall asleep on an adult learn to depend upon an adult to help them fall asleep, which in turn causes disruptions when they wake up in the middle of the night and cannot soothe themselves back to sleep.

See what works for your charges and go with that.

Children Sleep Needs Per Day

- *Newborns (up to three months): 14 to 17 hours.*

- *Infants (four to 11 months): 12 to 15 hours.*

- *Toddlers (one to two): 11 to 14 hours.*

- *Preschoolers (three to five): 10 to 13 hours.*

- *School-age (six to 13): 9 to 11 hours.*

- *Tweens and Teens (14 to 17): 8 to 10 hours.*

STAY AT HOME PRINCIPAL

Whether they are working or are taking a sick day, many principals now stay at home when the nanny is working. When a principal stays at home, it changes the power dynamic in the house. Charges will try to go over the nanny's head and defer to their parent every chance they get. Subside the stress of feeling as if you are working under a microscope by having a conversation with the at home principals to set clear boundaries for yourself and the charges. Then make sure these boundaries are clearly communicated to your charges. It may be best if the principals tell the charges what these boundaries are.

Common Boundaries with "Stay at Home" Principals.

- Inform charges at the beginning of the day when the principals will be ready to spend time with them.
- Decide who is in charge. Nanny or principal? It seems so simple but deciding whether the nanny is taking the lead or assisting the principal can relieve stress for the nanny, especially if the nanny is expected to keep the children on a schedule or set rules and discipline.

TALKING

One of the biggest advantages in childcare is being able to clearly communicate with children. Nannies are around for a lot of charge's firsts. Accurately explaining to children what they should expect, as well as how they are expected to act, in a situation they have never experienced before will soothe their anxieties and limit fears. The first day of school, getting vaccinated, and flying on a plane are all experiences a charge may want to know more about before they encounter them.

- *Listen and Let Charges Finish Speaking.*
  Don't be too quick to give a solution. Talk through whatever is on a charge's mind.

- *Point Out Positives.*
  Given the situation, agree that there may be negatives but that the positives outweigh them.

- *Embrace Charge's Fears.*
  Brushing off a charge's concern will inevitably lead to them resisting the experience or heighten their anxiety. Give charges concrete solutions to help them feel some control over the situation. Oftentimes letting a charge sit on your lap or hold your hand will be enough.

TANTRUMS

Charges that are quick to tantrum have been rewarded for doing so in the past by getting their way. A tantrum is a habit and changing habits will take time and dedication.

- *Evaluate the Situation.*

    Some charges may be set to scream if they aren't getting their way. However, the one justified reason for a child to resort to an outburst is when a they feel that their concerns have not been acknowledged. Avoid a tantrum set off from a caregiver's poor listening by explaining to a charge what is going on and saying, "I understand you want XYZ, but screaming for it is not the way to get it." Then a charge will feel heard and be sure to point out if you still do not understand what they are going through.

- *Do Not Negotiate.*

    Negotiating with a charge during their outburst reinforces their tantrum game plan. The tantrums were still worth it even if they only get a little bit of what they originally wanted.

- *Have a Redo.*

    A redo would be trying the whole situation over with the behavior you would have liked to have seen in place of the tantrum. Stop everything and try again if a child decides to have a tantrum in the store after you refused to get XYZ for them. Leave the cart and leave the store. Explain your expectation, that they appropriately ask and possibly not get XYZ. Then walk back in with the charge and pass by XYZ, to give them a chance to try this strategy.

    If the child is too hysterical to try a redo then leaving is still the first step and shows them that an outburst will not get XYZ.

- *Change Up Your Reaction and Method.*

Be wary of giving a charge the power in a tantrum by making the repercussion predicable. A charge may begin to understand that they have power by welcoming the consequence. In this case you may benefit from switching up the consequence from a time out to a privilege being taken away.

TIME OUT

There is no disciplinary technique as tried and true as a "time out." A time out is a break from the previous moment for both charges and adults. Time outs are a chance to cool off.

Time outs come in two parts.

1) Amount of time apart.

2) A conversation.

- *The Time.*

   Time outs do not have to be long to be effective. A misconception is a time out's length directly shows the charge how bad their actions were. Some say the length of a time out should be the age of a charge, three and a half years old = three and a half minutes.

   When I babysit a new child, depending on the age or maturity of the child, I start my time outs at two minutes and let them know that it increases by a minute or doubles for every time out after that. I also sometimes start time outs over if the charge moves from the time out spot and add a minute if they ask, "how much longer," or, "is it over yet?"

   Pick an appropriate spot for the time away, a chair, corner on the floor, or the bottom step of a staircase. However, if the child is small, a place where you cannot keep an eye on the little one, like a bedroom, is not ideal.

- *The Conversation.*

  A conversation about the unwanted incident must always follow a time out because a time out on its own doesn't teach any lessons, nor will a charge necessarily reflect on what has happened because they were put in one. Make sure to share your feelings.

  Time outs work for more than charges. Depending on the crime, taking a toy away and specifically saying that it is in time out will be enough to teach a charge a lesson in following rules. This also lets a charge know time outs are for everyone.

  Remember to put your smile back on when the time out is over. The time has been served and it is time to move on.

  Standing your ground, no matter what doesn't do anyone any favors. The moment you realize you went overboard is the moment to correct that misstep. Go to your charge and start the conversation about what happened and say you're sorry.

TRANSPARENCY

The glue that bonds principals and nannies is transparency. Transparency creates productivity, trust, and cultivates a happy workplace. Transparency also goes both ways.

Transparency is unbiased, unsugar-coated and sometimes ugly honesty. Equally discuss the failures as much as the fun when recapping the day's events to principals. If a charge was hurt, say exactly what happened, even if that means admitting you froze up or didn't see it.

Transparency is for more than sharing bad news and mishaps. It also creates engagement between the nanny and the principals, which in turn spurs understanding and enthusiasm. Speaking candidly develops trust and passion for the nanny, leading nannies to innovate and bring more of themselves to the position.

Two Keys to Transparency

- *Communicate arising issues before they become problems. Holding back ideas or concerns is demotivating and will slow down productivity.*

- *Meet with the principals daily or weekly to formally or informally share, problem solve, and create a sense of well-being and understanding.*

UNSOLICITED ADVICE

Be wary to give principals advice that they haven't asked for. It isn't the nanny's business to step in and consult with the principals, even if you notice the principals having a hard time getting their children to do something, when your way works 100% of the time for you. If principals want your advice, they will ask for it.

URGENT

Urgency is relative. Tasks often seem as if they must be done ASAP when in reality they don't. Relax and remember everything will get done if a family has allowed time for it. However, something is wrong if everything is easily put off.

VACATIONING WITH FAMILIES

Traveling with a family can be one of the toughest but most rewarding and worthwhile experiences a nanny can have. Even for nannies that constantly travel with a family it is a good idea to go over a game plan to figure out the schedule for the upcoming trip and what responsibilities will be expected of them. Ask for as much information as you need. Trips do not always go as planned, set yourself up for success with an open mind and being ready for last second changes.

- *Accommodations.*
  Nannies should absolutely weigh in and discuss their needs with principals. Many families will want their nanny to room with their charges but just as many will make sure their nanny is set up with their own room, hotel, or apartment.

- *On or Off the Clock?*
  Determining when you are on or off the clock can be tricky if you're constantly around the family. Be prepared with a game plan and a schedule. Discuss with the family before you're packed if you are being paid while on the plane and traveling.

- *Expenses.*

  A family's vacation is a nanny's work trip. Per diem is a common way for a family to help offset any of the nanny's personal expenses, such as meals and taxis, just like a work trip in any other industry. Other expenses may include groceries, luggage fees, ATM and currency exchange fees, and phone plans.

- *International Travel.*

  Aside from needing a passport, every country has its own entry requirements and fees for a family's nanny and domestic staff. Research and discuss what arrangements your nanny family has made for you and if you need to fill anything out.

VALUES

Teaching values is a partner project between the nanny and principals. Ask what habits, mindset, beliefs, and traits they would like to see in their children, then build a household culture together that instills them. If helping around the home is important to the principals, then a charge could practice setting the table before meals. If kindness is important, then a nanny may want to remind their charge to ask to touch something before they grab it, and encourage "please" and "thank you." However, nannies must have a conversation with the principals if they become the only one enforcing and encouraging these behaviors.

WAIT A MOMENT

Stop, breathe, and give yourself a moment to think. It is difficult for anyone to make a split-second decision and be confident that they made the right call. Waiting just a moment to think before speaking may be all the time needed to be confident that the choice you made will lead to the resolution you want.

Take a breath and give yourself a chance to think through the consequences of your decision before you overstep. Keep yourself from making a rash decision or giving an over the top punishment by taking a moment to pause and think before moving forward.

WEAPONS

Children are magicians when it comes to pretending and playing with toys. A stick can become a wand. A towel can be a cape. Anything can become a weapon and when it does, take it away. Teddy bear or baseball bat, I have a zero-tolerance rule; when something becomes a weapon, I take it away for the day. Children easily forget boundaries and usually think everyone is in on the fun. A quick warning goes a long way for everyone. Remind charges what is expected of them before they take something too far.

WHAT IS AFTER NANNYING?

I have struggled and wondered about my career as a nanny. What will I do when I'm older? The answer is simple: still be a nanny. A career as a nanny can last as long as you desire. A nanny is an honorable profession without an age limit. Many nannies wish to progress from nanny to teacher or use their talents with children to earn money while in school. However, there is room at the table for every nanny no matter the reason you became one. For those that are passionate about helping raise children, put the worries to bed, and accept that becoming a nanny may be the best career move you've made.

X FACTOR

That special, outstanding, indescribable quality, and extraordinary ability someone possesses is their X factor. Leaning into your natural fantastic qualities, whether you're enthusiastic, nurturing, punctual, organized, trustworthy, or communicative, may help you land your dream job with your perfect-fit family. The process is one of self-discovery, salesmanship, and often doubling down on sharping your nanny skill set by constantly seeking out knowledge to benefit your career. Actors take singing lessons, singers take dance lessons, and nannies take child development, cooking, and CPR classes.

Y

"YES, IF YOU HEAR ME"

It can feel like talking to a wall when a child is too distracted to respond, but that doesn't mean they aren't listening. If your only trouble when it comes to listening is getting a charge to acknowledge the information you've just given them, using the phrase, "say yes if you hear me," may do the trick.

Children aren't born knowing they are supposed to respond to information and telling a charge that you would like them to respond may help them understand that they are supposed to, but it might not change their behavior to do it.

Next time you and your charge are having a fantastic time at the park and you've just given the, "we are leaving in five minutes," but your charge hasn't responded, try "yes, if you hear me." Instead of calling your charge's name over and over again expecting for them to suddenly respond, announce, "say yes, if you hear me," and if they heard you, like a charm they will respond "yes."

"YOU CAN DO HARD THINGS"

Do you find yourself at odds with a charge unwilling to take on a challenge they are capable of and then you utter the phrase, "It's not that hard?"

Sometimes it is difficult to tell the difference between complaining and suffering. The phrase, "It's not that hard," belittles a charge when we truly want to empower them. Try switching to the empowering, "you can do hard things." This simple switch can change a charge's mood and belief in themselves.

"YOU'RE NOT IN TROUBLE"

It happens to every caregiver; your back was turned and a charge's scream lets you know something just happened between her and her brother. No matter what just happened, it can be a conundrum to unravel the, "he started it," "no, she started it," mess that just occurred.

Most of the time the fear of being in trouble is what keeps children from being honest. It is hard for children to fess up to something that might have been an accident when they believe they are going to be automatically blamed as if they did it purposefully.

Over the 14 years of being a camp director for four-year-olds to 15-year-olds, I discovered the universal truth that it is far easier to figure out what caused a situation between children when both parties feel that they are being heard. It comes down to the phrase "you're not in trouble, I just want to know what happened." After I uttered those words, instantly children opened up. Even the guilty ones would tell me what happened. Everyone just wanted to be heard. Children wanted the chance to say, "yes, I did something wrong but they hurt my feelings too." Give it a chance and see how easy it is to move past the "he said, she said."

Z

ZEN

Being a nanny is a tough job. Caring for someone else's child is not like most other occupations. It can also be a lonely job, having no other work place associates to confer with and speaking with a principal is similar to having a work place conversation with a CEO. Sometimes there is more to get done in a day than is possible. However, being a nanny can be extremely rewarding but finding a balance between fulfillment and feeling burdened may be a challenge.

Calming and relaxation strategies can help a nanny thrive. Zen is recognizing the joy of being, maintaining pure balance with a clear mind to face all challenges ahead, and freeing your mind to be accommodating, understanding, and adaptive to all obstacles. There is always time for a nanny to practice balance.

Intentional Breathing Exercise

1. Become aware of your stress level.

2. Intentionally slow your breathing with a deep breath in, counting in your head 1, 2, 3, 4.

3. Pause. This is not holding your breath, rather it is acknowledging the inhale.

4. Slowly release the breath, counting in your head 1, 2, 3, 4.

5. Pause to acknowledging the exhale.

6. Repeat four times or until the anxiety is reduced.

Do not exceed five minutes of Intentional Breathing. Stop if you become lightheaded or dizzy.

ZIG ZAG

Whether I was asking for time off or a raise, I have never found a situation to be as scary as I've imagined. I always imagine my employers being upset with me and that has never been the case. Every time I thought someone was going to zig, they zagged.

Sometimes a situation that seemed it was going to end up one way, turned out to go another I never even considered. I had to learn to go in and give every nerve-wracking situation a chance. I discovered my employers were never angry, rather they were impressed and glad that I shared my concerns and feelings. The more I spoke up, the easier it became to share my wants and needs, helping me to achieve more and become even more valuable to the family.

WORKS CITED

NAEYC, www.naeyc.org/our-work/families/
understanding-and-responding-children-who-bite.

Vistaprint.com, www.vistaprint.com/hub/design-decoded-top-12-easy-read-
fonts?couponAutoload=1&GP=05/16/2019 21:21:28&GPS=5385281956&GNF=0.

"10 Top Characteristics to Look For In A Nanny." *Mommy
Connections*, 7 June 2014, www.mommyconnections.ca/
blog/2012/10/22/10-top-characteristics-to-look-for-in-a-nanny/.

"15 Red Flags You Shouldn't Ignore on Your Next Interview." *WinterWyman*, winter-
wyman.com/blog/15-red-flags-you-shouldnt-ignore-your-next-interview.

"8 Things a Traveling Nanny Needs to Know." *Sittercity.
com*, 22 Apr. 2019, www.sittercity.com/sitters/
child-care-tips-sitters/8-things-a-traveling-nanny-needs-to-know.

"About CPI." *Crisis Prevention Institue*, www.crisisprevention.com/About-Us.

ADMIN, 906 ARS. *Red Light/Green Light*, www.gameskidsplay.net/games/
sensing_games/rl_gl.htm.

"Are Hidden Nanny Cams Actually Legal?" *The Reeves Law Group*, 14 Mar. 2016, www.
robertreeveslaw.com/blog/nanny-cams/.

"Au Pairs for Hire | Childcare Jobs." *GreatAuPair*, www.greataupair.com/nanny-
aupair-agency/AuPair-Nanny-Differences.htm.

Behance, Inc. "11 Ways to Avoid Burnout." *Adobe 99U*, 26 Feb. 2019, 99u.adobe.com/
articles/24201/11-ways-to-avoid-burnout.

"Benefits of Being Organized." *Benefits*, www.organizeyourlife.org/Benefits.htm.

Brawley, Lora, and Lora BrawleyLora. "Parent FAQ
Overview." *Nanny FAQ*, 17 Oct. 2014, nannyfaq.com/
playdate-etiquette-when-moms-and-nannies-come-together/.

Campbell, Sherrie. "10 Ways to Maximize Your Workday." *Entrepreneur*, 4 Feb. 2016,
www.entrepreneur.com/article/270331.

Care.com, Inc. "12 Child Care Training Courses And Certifications
That Will Boost Your Career." *Care.com*, www.care.com/c/
stories/2680/12-nanny-training-courses-and-certifications/.

Care.com, Inc. "Handling Nanny Vacations, Holidays And Sick Days." *Care.com*, www.
care.com/c/stories/3157/handling-nanny-vacations-holidays-and-sick-days/.

"Charge." *Merriam-Webster*, Merriam-Webster, www.merriam-webster.com/
dictionary/charge.

Cole, Samantha, and Samantha Cole. "9 Ways To Take More Initiative At
Work." *Fast Company*, Fast Company, 4 Dec. 2018, www.fastcompany.
com/3037092/9-ways-to-take-more-initiative-at-work.

"Communicating Well with Children: Tips." *Raising Children Network*, 5 June 2017, raisingchildren.net.au/toddlers/connecting-communicating/communicating/communicating-well-with-children.

Editors, The. "This Hidden Shoe Organizer Idea Is Seriously Genius." *Good Housekeeping*, Good Housekeeping, 25 Jan. 2019, www.goodhousekeeping.com/home/tips/g2610/best-organizing-tips/.

Education.com. "How to Play Simon Says | Activity." *How to Play Simon Says | Activity | Education.com*, 18 Mar. 2014, www.education.com/activity/article/simon/.

"Employment Rights of Nannies." *International Nanny Association*, nanny.org/resources/nannies/employment-rights-of-nannies/.

Food Network Kitchen. "8 Things You Should Never Put in the Dishwasher." *Food Com*, www.foodnetwork.com/recipes/packages/kitchen-fixes/things-you-should-not-put-in-dishwasher.

Graziano, P A, et al. "Maternal Behavior and Children's Early Emotion Regulation Skills Differentially Predict Development of Children's Reactive Control and Later Effortful Control." *Infant and Child Development*, U.S. National Library of Medicine, 1 July 2010, www.ncbi.nlm.nih.gov/pmc/articles/PMC3034150/.

Greenawald, Erin. "43 Resume Tips That Will Help You Get Hired." *Free Career Advice*, The Muse, 3 Dec. 2015, www.themuse.com/advice/43-resume-tips-that-will-help-you-get-hired.

Halstead, Josh. "5 Reasons Why First Aid Training Is Important." *SMRT Indiana*, SMRT Indiana, 31 Mar. 2014, www.smrtindiana.com/blog/2014/3/31/5-reasons-why-first-aid-training-is-important.

Halteman, Ed. "2017 INA Nanny Salary Benefits Survey." *Https://Nanny.org/Production/Wp-Content/Uploads/2018/01/2017-INA-Nanny-Salary-Benefits-Survey-FINAL.pdf*, International Nanny Association, 15 Dec. 2017.

"Handwashing - Clean Hands Save Lives | CDC." *Centers for Disease Control and Prevention*, Centers for Disease Control and Prevention, www.cdc.gov/handwashing/index.html.

Hickey, Kasey Fleisher, et al. "How Transparency at Work Can Help Your Team." *Wavelength by Asana*, 20 Nov. 2017, wavelength.asana.com/workstyle-transparency/.

"Home, Kitchen & Laundry Appliances & Products." *Whirlpool*, www.Whirlpool.com/.

"Household Payroll and Tax Services." *HomeWork Solutions*, www.homeworksolutions.com/.

"How Long Should Toddlers Nap." *Sleep.org*, www.sleep.org/articles/how-long-should-toddler-nap/.

"How Much Do I Pay a Nanny?" *Nanny Lane*, www.nannylane.com/guide/nanny/cost/cost.

"How to Do Laundry." *The New York Times*, The New York Times, www.nytimes.com/guides/smarterliving/how-to-do-laundry.

Howcast. "How to Play Hot and Cold." *WonderHowTo*, WonderHowTo, 12 Jan. 2010, kid-games.wonderhowto.com/how-to/play-hot-and-cold-285831/.

"Insurance Commissioner: Who Are They & Why Contact Them – CreakyJoints." *CreakyJoints*, creakyjoints.org/support/insurance-issues/insurance-commissioner/.

Joyce, Susan P. "How to Succeed at Interviews for a New Job." *Job*, Job Hunt, 29 Nov. 2018, www.job-hunt.org/job_interviews/job-interviewing.shtml.

LearnVest. "Red Flag Alert: 5 Signs You Shouldn't Take a Job." *Free Career Advice*, The Muse, 24 Feb. 2013, www.themuse.com/advice/red-flag-alert-5-signs-you-shouldnt-take-a-job.

"Nanny Annual Salary ($32,896 Avg | May 2019)." *ZipRecruiter*, www.ziprecruiter.com/Salaries/Nanny-Salary.

"Nanny Responsibilities & Job Descriptions." *NannyAuthority*, 26 Jan. 2016, nanny-authority.com/nanny-responsibilities/.

"Nanny Salary and Benefits Survey." *International Nanny Association*, nanny.org/resources/industry-services/salary-and-benefits-survey/.

"Nanny Service Tips for Traveling with Your Nanny." *Diamond Personnel*, 16 Mar. 2017, www.diamondpersonnel.com/family-blog/uncategorized/nanny-service-tips-traveling-nanny/.

Nieboer, Geof. "A.K.A. German Spotlight." *Flashlight Tag*, www.gameskidsplay.net/games/chasing_games/tag/tag_flashlight.htm.

"Organization." *Organization Dictionary Definition | Organization Defined*, www.yourdictionary.com/organization.

Perper, Rochelle. "Relaxation Exercises." *Http://Therapychanges.com/Pdf/Resources/RelaxationTechniques.pdf*, www.TherapyChanges.com. PSY 23090 5055 North Harbor Drive Suite 320 San Diego, CA 92106

Porter, Jane, and Jane Porter. "Why Our Brains Love Lists And How To Make Better Ones." *Fast Company*, Fast Company, 9 Jan. 2015, www.fastcompany.com/3040420/why-our-brains-love-lists-and-how-to-make-better-ones.

"Principal." *Merriam-Webster*, Merriam-Webster, www.merriam-webster.com/dictionary/principal.

"Psychiatric Advance Directives and Reduction of Coercive Crisis Interventions." *Taylor & Francis*, www.tandfonline.com/doi/abs/10.1080/09638230802052195.

Rivas, Emily. "10 Fun and Educational Games to Play with Toddlers." *Today's Parent*, 21 Feb. 2017, www.todaysparent.com/toddler/toddler-development/fun-games-to-play-with-toddlers/.

Ryan, Liz. "Ten Red Flags That Scream 'Do Not Take This Job'." *Forbes*, Forbes Magazine, 22 Jan. 2018, www.forbes.com/sites/lizryan/2018/01/22/ten-red-flags-that-scream-do-not-take-this-job/#395d8963277c.

Sachs, Lexie, and Good Housekeeping Institute. "5 Tips to Prevent Clothes from Pilling." *Good Housekeeping*, Good Housekeeping, 21 Mar. 2018, www.goodhousekeeping.com/institute/a19518/tips-preventing-clothing-pilling/.

Sapolsky, Barry S., and Barbara K. Kaye. "Taboo or Not Taboo? That Is the Question: Offensive Language on Prime-Time Broadcast and Cable Programming." *Journal of Broadcasting & Electronic Media*, vol. 53, no. 1, 2009, pp. 22–37., doi:10.1080/08838150802643522.

Shawncarterm. "Here's the Trick to 'Becoming Wealthy,' Says Author Who Studies Millionaires." *CNBC*, CNBC, 26 Oct. 2017, www.cnbc.com/2017/10/25/heres-the-trick-to-becoming-wealthy-says-tom-corley.html.

Singh, Aman. "Influencing Behavior: What Will It Take to Save 600,000 Lives a Year?" *Forbes*, Forbes Magazine, 11 Oct. 2012, www.forbes.com/sites/csr/2012/10/11/influencing-behavior-what-will-it-take-to-save-600000-lives-a-year/#46a1e31a3172.

"Six Things That Can Happen When Paying Your Nanny Under the Table." *GTM Household*, gtm.com/household/resource-center/paying-nanny-under-the-table/.

Stoker, John. "Why Don't People Take Initiative?" *DialogueWORKS*, www.dialogueworks.com/blog/why-don039t-people-take-initiative.

Supernanny. "Nine Ways to Make Them Listen." *Supernanny Parenting*, Supernanny, 24 July 2017, www.supernanny.co.uk/Advice/-/Parenting-Skills/-/Routine-and-Teamwork/9-ways-to-make-them-listen.aspx.

"Taking InitiativeMaking Things Happen in the Workplace." *Career Development From MindTools.com*, www.mindtools.com/pages/article/initiative.htm.